Awaken to Good Mour

Mark E. Hundley, M.Ed., L.P.C.

Foreword

This is a class that no one wants to take; however, it is a required course in the journey of life.

Most of us embrace denial and find ourselves faced with stark reality without the wherewithal to deal with the inevitable.

I did not want to write this. It meant that I would be forced to take on the unpleasant task of looking into the face of heartache, loss, and death.

Life, as it will do to all of us, dealt Mark the most painful of blows. But in *Awaken to Good Mourning*, he has transformed tragedy into something positive.

I admire Mark for what he has done and what he continues to do.

Ronnie Dunn

Dedication

This second edition of *Awaken to Good Mourning* would not be possible without the support I have received from so many! In honor of the invaluable influence and support so freely and generously given to me, I dedicate this volume to the following:

My wife Vanessa for her tireless support of all aspects of my work—I love you!

My daughter Kacie, the bravest young woman I know—I love you!

Chris Hay and Brandy Reeves—my "children on the blend"—you are the best!

Roy Austin, PhD—friend and therapist who helped save my life.

The late Byron Medler, EdD—Professor, mentor, and friend—you are always in my heart.

Ted Cantrell—my friend.

My fellow founders of the Journey of Hope Grief Support Center.

The children and families served by the Journey of Hope Grief Support Center.

Preface

This book is born from my own personal experiences with death, mourning, and recovery. I, like so many others in our society, was not prepared to face the excruciating pain associated with the death of a loved one when my first wife, Christy, died as a result of injuries she received in an automobile accident on January 24, 1989. I suddenly found myself the single father of a seven-year-old daughter. I was numb, angry, confused, frightened, and searching— searching for some kind of guidance and support to get through the tasks that lay ahead of me. Because of my professional background, I was fortunate to know how to access the assistance I so desperately needed; yet, I was aware of how much more difficult it would have been for my daughter and me had I not known where to turn. In the midst of my journey through the grieving process, I realized that there were certain holes in my experience that proved difficult to fill and suspected that if these holes were a part of *my* experience, they were likely a part of the experience of others as well.

As I worked through my grief, I learned many practical principles and discovered some very helpful resources around which I rebuilt my life. Convinced that individuals and families facing the devastating death of a loved one could benefit from these principles and resources as well, I developed *Awaken to Good Mourning* as a guide for personal journeys of grief. I do not claim that this volume contains all that is necessary for individuals and families to successfully negotiate the aftermath of the death of a loved one, but it does contain gleanings from my own pilgrimage through the grief process. May you find the information contained in these pages useful as you work through your own grief.

Introduction

Awaken to Good Mourning is divided into four major sections — three describing the process of mourning and one offering encouragement to set you on the path to your own good mourning journey. The four appendices contain unique resources for you to reference as you journey through grief.

I believe that framing the process of mourning in terms of phases rather than stages best describes the experiences common to mourners on this shared journey. The concept of stages tends to cause us to think in terms of linear and sequential movement through the process. This approach encourages us to believe that as we move out of a particular stage, we will not experience the emotions connected with that stage again. Nothing could be further from the truth! Reality tells us that mourners tend to float among and between various grief experiences, making the process fluid, not rigid and predictable. Some research has suggested that stage models may actually even hinder healthy movement through the process.

Viewing the process of mourning in phases, on the other hand, allows for the identification of various common experiences connected with mourning and, at the same time, provides a structure in which an overlapping and intertwining of those commonalities may occur.

The three phases of mourning I have recognized are:

- **Early Mourning — The Loss Event**

- **Mid-Mourning — The Transition**

- **Late Mourning — The Continuation**

Each section of the book contains discussions of *characteristics*, *challenges*, and *choices* most often identified in each unique phase.

Defining Terms

Throughout the book, you will notice references to the terms *grief work* and *grief process*. These terms are similar, yet refer to two distinct aspects of what you are facing. The grief process is made up of common experiences, emotions, thoughts, and response patterns encountered by individuals, families, and corporate bodies following the death of a loved one. In essence, *grief* is the combination of mental, emotional, relational, physical, and spiritual experiences common to the loss experience. In general terms, the process of grief can be observed, charted, conceptualized, and communicated in various formats to help clarify what you may experience as you deal with your loss.

The term *grief work*, on the other hand, refers to the specific activities you choose to employ as you mourn your loss. Grief work, or *mourning*, focuses on action steps taken in an effort to reconcile yourself to your loss and integrate it into the framework of your life as you continue living. Activities such as talking, writing, reading, support group participation, exercise, art, gardening, and counseling are all examples of grief work or *mourning*. Mourning is the personal, unique approach you choose to take in working through your loss.

Grief is the natural outgrowth of the loss event, while *mourning* is the process of acting upon and within those experiences—the goal being healthy reconciliation of those experiences into the whole of our lives! Mourning externalizes what is essentially an internal experience. Both grieving, or experiencing the commonalities of loss, and mourning, the process of making meaning through acts of choice, are essential for healthy reconciliation of loss.

Why 'Good Mourning'

The title of this book, *Awaken to Good Mourning*, reflects my intent to share the idea that the process of mourning the loss of your loved one *can* be healthy, positive, and healing! I believe that vast numbers of people do not experience healing from the pain of loss and, as a result, never experience the healthy, positive aspects of this process. These negative experiences with grief and loss may be referred to as *bad mourning*.

Bad mourning experiences tend to bring about compounded and complicated grief and can cause unreconciled loss to build up in our lives. Societal injunctions, family rules, and personal belief systems tend to reinforce bad mourning habits. As a whole, our society does not deal well with death, dying, and grief; therefore, we have become inundated with messages that promote quick fixes, unrealistic expectations, and disconnected support strategies.

Bad mourning habits often deny the reality of loss and its effects on the person or family and repress emotions and thoughts related to the pain of loss. Bad mourning may find its expression through over involvement in activities such as work, social causes, spending and shopping, travel, religion, sexual activity, or alcohol or drug use—which are all intended to medicate or numb us from the pain and loneliness brought on by loss.

My experience as a therapist tends to verify how pervasive bad mourning is as people seek to cope with loss. Bad mourning not only hinders healing and reconciliation, it may potentially color every aspect of your life, affecting your relationships, career, physical health, mental health, and emotional well-being.

Good mourning, on the other hand, asserts that you can experience healing and emerge healthier and more complete as a result. Good mourning is not a magical shortcut through the grief process. It is not an easy way out of your pain. Rather, it is the process of honestly facing the reality of your loss, coming to terms with its impact on your life, learning to access all available resources for your recovery, and continuing to live productively as a result of the process.

The concept of good mourning may run contrary to the norm in your life where loss is involved. Perhaps for the first time, you may find yourself embracing the idea that mourning loss can indeed be a good, healthy, healing experience. You may find yourself entering into a new way of thinking, feeling, and acting. The possibility of good mourning experiences can shed new light on the necessary tasks of mourning that lie ahead of you.

Obviously, facing the tasks associated with good mourning presents certain levels of difficulty. This book will address each task by providing practical, understandable, and useful information and resources which you may continually revisit throughout the grief process.

Identifying Bad Mourning

In reading this book, you should keep in mind some common strategies of bad mourning which are routinely tied to typical coping mechanisms. Each coping mechanism in and of itself is perfectly normal and may be experienced at any time in your grief walk. However, when these reactions to your loss continue unchecked or become the primary strategy used in your grief work, they can keep you from picking up the pieces and moving on with your life. Therein lies the danger.

As you approach the tasks of mourning, consider ways to make your experience healthier. Reflect on these warning signs of bad mourning and look for ways to avoid their traps as you move on to your personal good mourning experience. I urge you to refer to this section occasionally as a way of keeping yourself on the positive track to recovery. An evaluative questionnaire is provided at the end of this section to assist in the monitoring process.

1. *Denial and Projection*—People who use denial or projection as a primary strategy of coping may think things like, "These things happen to others, not to me!" "I don't have to deal with this right now." "If I ignore this, it will go away." If you choose to use this style of coping, you may run the risk of living in a created reality in which the rules of the game may be changed any time a threat to this false reality is perceived. This approach allows you to keep running from circumstances. Eventually, the reality of the situation *will* break through, resulting in extreme difficulty with confronting your loss. This could unnecessarily compound and complicate your mourning efforts. The state of Denial may be a good place to visit from time to time, but it is not a great place in which to live.

2. *Fear and Pessimism*—In your grief, you might hear yourself saying something like, "I hope that these things (death, sickness, loneliness, etc.) will not happen to me, but I am afraid they will." "The world is a dangerous place; I must be careful and not take risks." If you choose to use this system as your primary pattern in facing grief, you may end up developing a type of emotional, spiritual, and relational paralysis. Fear and pessimism can cause you to stay within the confines of the familiar and comfortable, even when those confines are harmful to your emotional, mental, or relational well-being. Unnecessary isolation and loneliness may result from the paralyzing effects of fear and pessimism.

3. *Trade-off and Bargaining*—Have you ever thought something like: "If I am good (pray, give money, help the poor, etc.), then bad things will not happen to me!" "I will make a deal with God (the universe, the stars, the cards, etc.), and everything will be okay!" Consistent use of this system can lead to magical thinking—thought processes that tend to ignore rational cause-and-effect relationships—thinking that ultimately keeps us from the power of personal choice. If you are not careful, you could be duped into believing that certain activities, promises, or associations will keep tragedy, pain, and grief away from your life or provide you with guarantees of security, health, and wealth. This system can serve to set you up for huge disappointments when a particular deal or supposed guarantee does not work out as promised. It may force you to seek false security from other deals, formulas, or gurus. You may find yourself hopping from one promise to another without any real relief in your grief experiences.

4. *Fatalism and Hopelessness*—Sometimes people say, "Bad things are going to happen to me anyway, so why fight them?" or "Nothing ever goes my way; I am just doomed to live like this!" If you routinely employ this system, you may discover that depression is a constant companion. I am not talking about acute depression associated with the loss of a loved one, a common experience in the grief process. The depression to which I refer here is the kind that may lead to addictive activities and behaviors intended to medicate the feelings of loneliness and helplessness associated with loss. Often, drug and alcohol abuse emerge from this type of approach, further reinforcing the apparent futility of life and inhibiting your ability to recover and integrate loss into the fabric of your life. Forget the debate between the glass being half-empty or half-full; in this system, there *is* no glass!

5. *False Guilt*—Grieving individuals often say, "What did I do to cause this to happen?" "If I had only said (done, known, heard, etc.) something else, this would not have happened!" "It's all my fault!" If you consistently operate within this particular system, you run the risk of developing a delusion of reference where everything that happens somehow relates to something you either did or did not do. You may truly feel responsible for things over which you had absolutely no control. This is false guilt! The comical side of this system is something in which we have all found ourselves at one time or another. For instance, how many times have you said, "Well, I washed my car so it is bound to rain!" as if there were a rain cloud floating around the sky looking specifically for *your* car! That is ridiculous and you may laugh at the notion, but it is not so comical for one to feel responsible for everything terrible that happens in life. This false guilt can become an impossible burden to bear and could possibly lead to self-destructive behaviors.

6. *Glorification and Martyrdom*—Loss can also lead one to say, "All of my struggles and pain show that I am living the way I am supposed to be (the way God wants me to live, according to his will)." "This is just my row to hoe, and I'll do the best I can." "This is my cross to bear (accompanied by a deeply meaningful sigh)." Notice the use of extreme or absolute statements such as the word "all." If you choose to consistently employ this system, you may develop a genuine martyr complex and take pride in just how much pain and suffering you can endure. You may find yourself throwing perpetual pity parties in order to gain sympathy from others. One disadvantage to this system is that you might find yourself working to maintain revolving groups of partygoers, since being around one who regularly throws them can be a drain on patience and compassion. If you find yourself in this type of existence, you may feel extreme sadness because there is no joy or possibility in life—only pain and pity!

7. *Evil and Warfare* — Be careful if you hear yourself saying, "Everything that happens to me is the result of some unseen warfare over which I have no control!" Again, take note of the absolute, "everything." This is another extremist stance that allows you to blame someone or something else for all the problems you encounter in life. The ultimate result of using this system is that you do not have to take responsibility for your own choices or life! Obviously there are events that occur outside of your control, but *everything*? You *do* have control over your responses to the things that happen to you. This system seeks to eliminate all personal responsibility in life and makes human beings puppets in some cosmic play. The result can be living constantly in the role of a victim — a place where hope and possibility do not dwell.

Again, you may from time to time find yourself using statements similar to the ones I have listed for you. It is only natural to experience some of these sentiments occasionally and make statements similar to the ones detailed; however, the dangers grow when a particular unhealthy system becomes your primary avenue to approach the process of mourning.

The major difference between the effects of bad mourning habits and good mourning strategies **is whether you are moving toward healthy living or** finding yourself stuck in patterns of behavior that restrict your freedom to heal. In an effort to assist you in monitoring your progress, I have included the following questionnaire that will help you assess your thoughts, statements, and actions. Please feel free to refer to it periodically as you conduct your work of mourning. I suggest that you either use a pencil to complete the questionnaire so that you can erase and retake it or copy your answers on a separate sheet of paper. Using a separate sheet of paper might provide you with a running record of your progress. You may also make copies of the assessment if you wish.

Good Mourning–Bad Mourning Assessment

Circle the answer that most accurately reflects your thoughts, feelings, statements and actions over the most recent seven-day period.

1. *I feel numb and experience difficulty believing the loss has occurred.*

1	2	3	4	5
Not at all	A Little	Somewhat	Frequently	Constantly

2. *I experience denial and an inability to accept that the loss is real.*

1	2	3	4	5
Not at all	A Little	Somewhat	Frequently	Constantly

3. *I experience delusional thoughts related to this loss.*

1	2	3	4	5
Not at all	A Little	Somewhat	Frequently	Constantly

4. *I am distracted by thoughts of this loss.*

1	2	3	4	5
Not at all	A Little	Somewhat	Frequently	Constantly

5. *I am preoccupied with and long for my deceased loved one.*

1	2	3	4	5
Not at all	A Little	Somewhat	Frequently	Constantly

6. *I find myself preoccupied with thoughts of death and/or suicide.*

1	2	3	4	5
Not at all	A Little	Somewhat	Frequently	Constantly

7. *I find that my sleep patterns are disrupted.*

1	2	3	4	5
Not at all	A Little	Somewhat	Frequently	Constantly

8. *I experience frequent nightmares, intrusive flashbacks, and/or memories of the loss event.*

1	2	3	4	5
Not at all	A Little	Somewhat	Frequently	Constantly

9. I experience insomnia.

	1	2	3	4	5
	Not at all	A Little	Somewhat	Frequently	Constantly

10. I feel restless and easily distracted.

	1	2	3	4	5
	Not at all	A Little	Somewhat	Frequently	Constantly

11. I suffer from panic attacks.

	1	2	3	4	5
	Not at all	A Little	Somewhat	Frequently	Definitely

12. I experience an overwhelming sense of hopelessness and emptiness.

	1	2	3	4	5
	Not at all	A Little	Somewhat	Frequently	Constantly

13. I experience waves of sadness and tearfulness.

	1	2	3	4	5
	Not at all	A Little	Somewhat	Frequently	Constantly

14. I experience fits of uncontrollable crying.

	1	2	3	4	5
	Not at all	A Little	Somewhat	Frequently	Constantly

15. I experience feelings of persistent, debilitating depression.

	1	2	3	4	5
	Not at all	A Little	Somewhat	Frequently	Constantly

16. I become upset and angry over the loss event.

	1	2	3	4	5
	Not at all	A Little	Somewhat	Frequently	Constantly

17. I experience pronounced anger and express aggressive behavior over this loss event.

	1	2	3	4	5
	Not at all	A Little	Somewhat	Frequently	Constantly

18. *I experience guilt resulting in my participation in self-destructive behaviors.*

1	2	3	4	5
Not at all	A Little	Somewhat	Frequently	Constantly

19. *I have a loss of interest in normal activities and routines.*

1	2	3	4	5
Not at all	A Little	Somewhat	Frequently	Constantly

20. *I avoid activities and people related to my loss event.*

1	2	3	4	5
Not at all	A Little	Somewhat	Frequently	Constantly

21. *I lack the mental and physical strength and focus to perform day-to-day activities.*

1	2	3	4	5
Not at all	A Little	Somewhat	Frequently	Constantly

Once you have completed this assessment, add up your scores and compare them with the guide provided below. Remember that the purpose of this assessment is to help you distinguish between your use of good mourning strategies versus bad mourning habits as you move through the grief process.

Good Mourning–Bad Mourning Assessment Scoring

Good Mourning	Moderately Good Mourning	Bad Mourning
21–70	71–90	91–105

As stated earlier, any of the reactions detailed in the previous paragraphs are perfectly common in the aftermath of a death loss. You may find yourself experiencing one or a combination of these reactions rather frequently early on—that is to be expected. That being the case, your scores might reflect a leaning toward bad mourning habits the first time you take the assessment. If this is the case, please do not automatically decide that you are stuck in bad mourning habits. The danger does not lie in experiencing normal reactions to loss. The danger comes when these normal reactions become primary systems when dealing with your loss.

The goal is for you to employ good mourning strategies that will help you experience reconciliation of your loss, thereby freeing you to continue living in healthy ways. As you experience healing through your mourning and continue to revisit this assessment, your scores will likely reflect that progress. Ultimately, you can expect your scores to move toward the good-mourning end of the continuum.

I hope that as you read this book, you will embrace it as a cherished and valued companion—a resource to which you will turn often while you work through your loss. Allow yourself to read, reflect, review, and re-read the information contained here as often as necessary—and share it with friends and family members as well.

Early Mourning — The Loss Event

The Loss Event, the death of your loved one, has caused your life to change drastically! Whether you have had time to prepare for the death, as in a long-term illness, or the experience came about suddenly and unexpectedly, things as you knew them will never be the same again. I know that this reality is not a pleasant one to face, but it is one from which there is no escape. *Life has changed!* Right now, you may be feeling an almost overwhelming sense of loss and misdirection. This is to be expected at a time like this.

Because of the Loss Event, you find yourself in the beginnings of the grief process, or the Early Mourning Phase. During this time, you will likely receive encouragement and support from friends and family while you begin facing your grief and making many important decisions following the death of your loved one. Although there is no guarantee that you have an established support system, most people do have a network of family, friends, or co-workers from which to draw support.

I encourage you to lean heavily on those who make up your current support system. Perhaps you have a best friend, neighbor, or social group from which you can draw strength. Most people have a desire to be a source of help during times like this. Although you are facing a personal loss, you do not have to be alone in the process. You might find it useful to share this book with those closest to you so that they can have a better idea of the situations ahead of you and feel more at ease as they work to be your companion on your personal journey of grief.

The Characteristics of Early Mourning

The process of grieving and mourning the loss of a loved one can be very difficult at times and is often complicated. You may experience a wide variety of emotions as you mourn this loss. The emotions described in this phase of grief are merely representative and tend to be the primary ones felt in the Early Mourning Phase. Just because we discuss an emotion as it relates to this particular phase does not mean that it is unique to just this phase. You may well experience any emotion mentioned here in another phase as well. The overlapping of various emotions often occurs as you move through each phase of this process. As you read on, you may be able to grasp some knowledge of what you can expect as you begin the work of mourning your loss. This can serve to ease some of the discomfort and fear that often accompanies entering into the process of grief.

Shock and a Feeling of Numbness

Initially, a strong sense of shock and feelings of numbness may occur. These are common experiences and may provide you with a sort of cushion from the pain and reality of your loss. Shock and numbness can serve to allow your mind to catch up with the brutal physical reality of what you have experienced and prepare you to move through the funeral and the first few weeks of the Early Mourning Phase of your grief.

Mechanical Responses

Closely related to the initial shock and numbness is the phenomenon of responding to daily tasks and demands in mechanical ways. Some have described the experience as feeling like a wind-up toy as they move through a daily routine that has become much different from their former one. Early on, this can be a sort of blessing in disguise.

In the hours and days following the death of your loved one, and prior to the actual funeral itself, others may perceive your responses as rather robotic in nature. So often, people who do not understand this part of the grieving process will comment on how strong you are or how well you are doing. They may not be aware of what is actually taking place inside you. Early on, there may be a lack of readily observable emotions, which may give others the false impression that everything is moving along well for you. The truth is that your body, mind, and emotions are protecting and insulating you from the horrible pain of your loss in order to allow you to move steadily into the reality of the process.

Disbelief and Denial

A sense of disbelief and denial of the reality of your situation is also a natural part of the early phase of this process. It is so difficult to come to grips with the fact that one whom you loved so much is no longer with you physically. Feelings of disbelief and denial are signs that you are beginning to grapple with the harsh reality you face. You want things to be different—you want them to go back to the way they were. You may even feel that you are in a dream from time to time, one from which you will soon wake up and all will be back to normal. Unfortunately, you are not in a dream and the reality of your loss demands attention.

Mourners have often found courage to embrace the pain of their losses by routinely repeating something like, "I find it hard to believe that this has happened to me!" Sharing this sentiment with those in your support system routinely opens the door **for shar**ing other thoughts and feelings related to your situation, and sharing creates healing.

Confusion and Disorientation

Yet another characteristic of the Early Mourning Phase is the sense of confusion and disorientation you may experience periodically. These feelings are common components of this phase of grief, and each individual can experience them in different ways based on a number of variables. Questions as to why this tragedy had to happen to you and your family, how you will be able to go on without your loved one, and how you will face the many changes ahead of you are common ones asked during this time. Please give yourself permission to ask such questions—they can open the door for you to begin to deal with your loss in healthy ways.

Do not expect yourself to have everything together or have all the answers. It is perfectly normal to feel confused and disoriented, to be devoid of answers. Answers to your questions will likely arrive in time as you learn to work through your feelings of grief in healthy, healing ways.

Isolation and Withdrawal

You may also experience the desire and need to isolate yourself or withdraw from decisions, people, responsibilities, and pressures for a while. This too is a common response to the initial distress of dealing with the loss of a loved one. The ability to withdraw for reflection and introspection can be helpful as you seek to determine the directions most beneficial for you and your family. Embrace these times and help others who care about you to understand that the desire to pull away from time to time is common and not out of the ordinary. This isolation can be a source of strength for you as you seek to use alone time to begin to get in touch with your personal thoughts and feelings.

Anger and Betrayal

During this early phase of your grief, you may also experience feelings of anger and betrayal. Your anger may be closely connected to the "why" questions mentioned earlier. You may be angry with God, yourself, a doctor, the situation, another relative, or someone connected with the loss of your loved one. You may also feel that life has betrayed you in some way. This sense of betrayal often relates to the shattered dreams, goals, hopes, and plans you may have shared with your loved one. You may even feel betrayed by or angry with your loved one for leaving you behind.

These feelings of anger and betrayal are perfectly normal and are to be expected. Work to find healthy and helpful ways to express your feelings without getting down on yourself if you occasionally express them in unhealthy ways. Expressing your anger verbally by saying something like, "I am so ANGRY that this has happened! I don't deserve this!" tends to give healthy vent to the energy swimming around inside you. Engaging in physical activity such as walking, running, gardening, or weight lifting, is also a way to release the energy associated with anger. Work to avoid doing or saying something that might hurt you or another person. If you do occasionally lose it, people around you will likely understand and be supportive of your need to express your emotions during this time. We will take a closer look at anger in the Characteristics of Mid-Mourning.

The loss of your loved one has caused you to enter into the grief process, a process that may be partially or wholly unfamiliar. You have briefly explored some of the experiences that are characteristic of this Early Mourning Phase of the process:

- **Shock and a Feeling of Numbness**

- **Mechanical Responses**

- **Disbelief and Denial**

- **Confusion and Disorientation**

- **Isolation and Withdrawal**

- **Anger and Betrayal**

As you move into this process, you are encouraged to share your feelings openly with those who make up your immediate support system. You may even want to share this book with them so that they might be able to support you more completely along the way.

~~~

That's for Christy! That random, disconnected thought pierced my consciousness the moment I heard the siren in the distance! A sense of panic and dread entered my soul. I did my best to shove the thought to the back of my mind—with little success. She had been gone only ten minutes; she should have been to work by then. Still, that nagging, gnawing uneasiness persisted.

I went about the tasks of preparing for my day and helping Kacie get ready for hers. That day was "Brownie Day" for Kacie, so she was dressed in her Brownie uniform and—appropriately, I might add—having a brownie and milk for breakfast. One more normal, routine day awaited all of us . . . and yet . . .

~~~

The phone rang and free-floating anxiety gripped my heart! ***"Accident? Where?"*** Anxiety ramped up to panic! *"Is she okay?"* Images of where Christy could have had an accident on her way to work flashed through my mind, none of them good! *"Yes, I'll get there as quickly as I can!"* I couldn't believe my ears! An accident! Ambulance! Hospital! Urgency! *How could this happen?* I asked myself.

Noise from behind caused me to turn around. Kacie had heard my conversation—the brownie and milk hit the floor. She was curled in a fetal position on our bed, crying—she needed me—she needed her mommy!

Taking her into my lap, I made three calls—one to Christy's parents, one to Kacie's school, and a third to my friend and life insurance agent, Ted Cantrell—all the while doing my best to comfort her and tell her everything was going to be okay. *"Everything is going to be OK . . ."* If only I could say that with confidence.

~~~

I drove as rapidly as possible across town to the hospital as waves of anger, disbelief, confusion, and anxiety swept over me. Visions of Kacie's sweet face contorted by fear as I left her at her school with her school counselor filled my mind's eye, causing my heart to ache. I drove and thought, drove and prayed, drove and . . .

What had she done? Wasn't she paying attention? Was she okay? Why this? Why now? Why us? God!

Hospital parking lot. Ambulance under the canopy—Christy's? Patient liaison waiting for me. Ushering me into a waiting room.

"The doctors are doing all they can! The best we have are working with her. We've already lost her twice, but she's a fighter! I'll keep you posted. I'm so sorry."

Somewhere else—that's all I wanted, just to be somewhere else! Almost without thinking, I began making calls to friends, family, and co-workers—sharing the news, asking for prayers, hoping that I was dreaming. I wasn't and I knew it!

~~~

Amidst crowds of people who had arrived to provide support in the hour or so I had been at the hospital, the doctor entered the room. All noise faded away. Anticipation and hope filled the faces of all present. What was the verdict?

"Mr. Hundley, I'm so sorry to tell you this . . . there's no easy way to tell you, but your wife is dead!"

His words hit me with the force of a brick wall, and I collapsed face-first on the floor between the sofa and telephone table in the room. I was crushed, devastated, disbelieving! All I wanted to do was disappear into the floor beneath me never to reappear.

"Mark, get up, get up. It will be okay. It will be okay." God bless those friends and family members doing their best to comfort and support me!

It would NEVER be okay again . . . EVER! Didn't they know that? Lies! All lies! I suddenly found myself looking down on myself from an upper corner of the room—surveying a surreal scene! *That has to be someone else on the floor! That's not me! This is not happening—not to me! Oh God!*

I later understood that I had a dissociative experience, something that can happen in extreme times of stress. I was brought to my senses and back to myself by an internal prompting to get up and start doing the next things that had to be done. I sat on the sofa and talked with the doctor—numb, confused, and mechanical—going through the motions.

~~~

"Daddy, how's Mommy?"

Kacie's sweet, timid voice wrested me from the emotional and mental fog in which I floundered. I motioned for my precious seven-year-old daughter to sit in my lap. I held her close and kissed the top of her head. I took a deep, ragged breath and began.

"Kacie, Mommy won't be coming home with us again. Mommy's body was hurt too badly in the accident and it won't work anymore. Kacie, Mommy's dead!"

Those words shook her as they had me and she wept silently, her body convulsing with each sob. The two most difficult tasks I had ever faced—telling my daughter that her mother was dead and holding her, knowing that I could do nothing to eliminate her pain—caused me to teeter on the brink of despair. Then her question . . .

"What do we do now, Daddy? Big question for such a small child!

"Kacie, I'm not sure what we are going to do, but I do know this, we have our faith, we have our family and friends and we have each other, and we're going to make it. We're going to make it!" Thus, our journey toward good mourning began.

~~~

Questions for Reflection

- How has your life changed because of your loss?

- With whom do you feel most comfortable sharing your thoughts right now?

- What is the most difficult part of the situation you face right now?

- What is the most important thing you need those in your support system to know right now?

The Challenges of Early Mourning

Generally, the Early Mourning Phase lasts from the time you learn about the death of your loved one through the final disposition of the body. For some, this period can extend as long as three to six weeks after the funeral. In other rare circumstances, this period can hang on and blend with other phases for years; however, this is not the norm. During this time, three unique challenges await your attention:

Getting through the Funeral

The first challenge is that of getting through the funeral. Within a few hours after the notification of the death, funeral arrangements are made. This can be an extremely stressful time for you and your family. Contact with a funeral director will take place at the funeral home itself or in your own home. Decisions regarding the type of service and who will officiate as well as the location of the service, visitation or calling hours, and the method of final disposition of the body are all part of this process. Next comes the contacting of family members, friends, and co-workers as well as the publishing of the obituary in the local newspaper.

Typically, there is a span of a few days from the time of death to the actual funeral, although in some faiths, final disposition of the body comes much sooner. Concerned, caring, and loving individuals will likely contact you with their condolences and offers of assistance during this initial period of mourning. Allow them to care for and nurture you and your family. This outpouring of help and love is a vital part of the mourning rituals necessary for the beginnings of healthy grief reconciliation.

The day of the funeral can be a very difficult one for everyone involved. It is a time to say good-bye to your loved one. The feelings of pain, loneliness, despair, and loss can be almost indescribable. Anticipate that these emotions may overwhelm you. Do not feel badly about your need to express those feelings through tears, hugs, and words. Give yourself permission to express your sense of loss in any way you feel comfortable.

"Getting through" the funeral is probably the best way to describe the first challenge in the Early Mourning Phase. You will have to plow through it in the best way you possibly can. No matter how much care and planning goes into the actual funeral service, it can be extremely difficult. You are saying good-bye to a loved one for the last time.

At this time, care and support from friends and family members can be of utmost importance. Do not be afraid to lean heavily on them for emotional, mental, spiritual, and physical support. Ask for what you need from those around you who are willing and able to give. During this time, people are most willing to assist you—they want to help. Let them! In so doing, you will find support as you embrace the first challenge of the Early Mourning Phase—getting through the funeral.

Dealing with First Things

Following the funeral, the second challenge of the Early Mourning Phase awaits your consideration—that of dealing with the "first things" necessary to put all of your loved one's affairs in order. These tasks will demand your attention. You may find that you need the assistance of a caring, understanding, and knowledgeable friend or family member to help organize all the details ahead of you. Again, this is a perfect time to ask for and accept help. The shock and numbness will likely still be present to a certain degree as you begin making calls and writing the letters required to settle estate matters, insurance issues, Social Security claims, and so forth.

During this period of activity, your focus will most likely fall on taking care of details which may not give you as much time to work on the emotional aspects of your personal grief. On the other hand, you may welcome some of the distraction as you continue to ease into the realities surrounding your loss. Work at reframing this activity period as one of the steps that must be taken in the process of mourning your loss.

Handling these details may provide you with a sense of closure and, at times, a unique sense of closeness to your loved one. This time may also give you the opportunity to reflect on your relationship with your loved one — a relationship that now exists in memory only and not active engagement. Many of these memories may be positive and uplifting. While taking care of details, you may find yourself both crying and laughing as you share your thoughts and memories with friends and family members. This sharing can form the foundation of your continued grief work as you move through the mourning process.

Not all relationships are perfect and you may discover some mental and emotional dissonance as you reflect. Do not be afraid of seemingly contradictory emotions and thoughts — these are common for persons facing a loss. Make note of these feelings, thoughts, and experiences and then plan to talk with someone about them as soon as possible. Realize that as you face this challenge, you will not only bring a measure of closure to some aspects of your grief, you will also begin opening the door to the next steps in your personal journey of grief.

Preparing for the Transitions to Come

The third challenge facing you in the Early Mourning Phase is that of preparing for the transitions ahead. Following the harried activity surrounding the funeral and the almost constant attention that you will likely receive from people who care for you, you will naturally move into a period of adjustment without your loved one. As much as you might want the whole world to recognize that your life has changed forever and to give you time to stop and make adjustments, the reality remains that life goes on.

Those who hovered so closely to you in the early days after the loss, as well as those who helped you handle the details of settling the affairs of your loved one will get back to their routine; that is to be expected. Now comes the beginning of a period of transitions and intense grief work. Although you can receive help from friends, family members, support groups, and professional counselors and therapists, the grief work ahead is yours alone.

This third challenge is possibly the most important of the Early Mourning Phase in that as you face it, you are preparing yourself to make necessary choices in the mourning process. Know that transitions await you. As you approach them, realize too, that you have choices and options for how you navigate them. This can provide you with a certain sense of freedom and personal empowerment as you move through the process of mourning your loss.

The mental preparation associated with Early Mourning includes facing certain challenges unique to this phase. The importance of facing them honestly and openly cannot be emphasized enough. The three challenges you face in Early Mourning are:

- **Getting through the Funeral**
- **Dealing with First Things**
- **Preparing for the Transitions to Come**

~~~

This isn't supposed to happen now—down the road a long while, but not now! Those were my thoughts as I walked through the casket room at the funeral home after having visited with the funeral director in her office. I was numb as we drove through the cemetery to select the plot for burial. How quickly my life had changed! Only that morning, Christy and I had discussed plans for the coming weekend. It just wasn't fair!

I decided that the funeral would take place two days from the day of her death—Thursday. I returned home and sat in semidarkness as the daylight waned in the early evening hours of a late January day. Everything was a blur, nothing made sense. The phone rang, jarring me out of my trance—a college friend calling to extend his condolences. That call forced me to continue making calls to folks around the country. *This will not be easy!*

~~~

Wednesday found me visiting with Kacie about the funeral. I knew enough to include her in as much of the planning as possible. She actually helped select the songs for the service as well as the clothes she wanted to see her mother dressed in for the service. Involving her in those processes created a bond that defies description.

Late that afternoon, I went to the funeral home to view Christy's body and finalize arrangements. I met the minister there, and we visited at length about the service. I was grateful for his presence, empathy, and attention. I needed that. Before I could go home to change, people began arriving for the viewing. Dressed in blue jeans and boots, I greeted each visitor—no one seemed to notice. How I was dressed seemed so insignificant at that time.

~~~

The day of the funeral was and still is a bit of a blur. The major recollections I have of that day revolve around my desire to pay attention to the needs of those around me—Kacie, my in-laws, my parents and relatives, Christy's students. The service was beautiful—I later listened to the tape. The sanctuary was full—more people than I could recall ever seeing at a funeral! The greeting line was long and exhausting. The graveside was cold and sobering. Emptiness started in the pit of my stomach, spreading rapidly to fill my insides as I dropped the final rose on the casket and turned to leave. I had made it through the funeral—barely so—but made it nonetheless.

~~~

The first of many realizations that life is too easily reduced to black and white came when I signed the papers at the funeral home finalizing arrangements. After the funeral, there were letters to write, phone calls to make, forms to fill out, and claims to **file.** Auto insurance, life insurance, credit card companies, employers, bills for services rendered—all those forms and more required my attention. With each signature, each call, my need to make sure that Christy's legacy exceeded the information spelled out in black and white grew in intensity.

I discovered that I was able to extract meaning from each form completed, each call made and each task handled, meaning that demanded further attention. I took note of the ideas generated, lessons learned, and insights gained as I worked steadily at handling the first things necessary after her death. I also found myself reminiscing about our life together and in those moments, I both laughed and cried.

~~~

Questions for Reflection

- How are you most comfortable expressing your sadness right now?

- What made or will make the funeral most meaningful for you and your family?

- Do you have a trusted friend whom you plan to invite to help you organize your thoughts and take care of the details associated with the death of your love one? Who is that person? When will you contact this person? What makes this person best suited for this task?

- As you look ahead, what specific transition do you feel *least* prepared to face?

- In like manner, what specific transition do you feel *most* prepared to face?

The Choices of Early Mourning

Death causes us to face our mortality in a way no other experience does. When touched by the death of a loved one, the myth of being in control is brutally shattered. You may suddenly feel extremely vulnerable, weak, and victimized. This sense of being out of control can be so overwhelming at times that it can paralyze your thoughts, feelings, and actions. Although you cannot control what life gives you, you *can* choose your responses.

In making choices, you begin regaining a sense of control over life in different ways than you had prior to the death. This sense of control can help you focus on how you respond to life's events. It can help you look at yourself and your life more realistically.

You are not a helpless victim in the path of an unmerciful world, steamrolled by its hit-and-run tactics. You can become more proactive as you handle challenges, taking responsibility for yourself and life. You can make a difference for yourself and others as you begin to make choices.

The Early Mourning Phase carries three unique choices that must be pondered—the Choice of Acknowledgement, Acceptance, and Affirmation; the Choice to Mourn the Loss Fully; and the Choice to Embrace the Pain of Mourning.

The Choice of Acknowledgement, Acceptance, and Affirmation

This first choice is one that begins almost at an unconscious level after you learn of the death of your loved one, and it has three components:

Acknowledgement requires moving the reality of the death of your loved one from the unconscious to the conscious processes of your thinking. Although shock and numbness surround you initially, life demands that you begin to acknowledge your loss in tangible ways.

We have already briefly addressed a couple of activities that will provide avenues for acknowledgement: The first of those is talking about what has happened, telling your story. The more you recount what has taken place, the better you will feel. I encourage you to share your story as often as possible and with as many who are willing to listen. A second activity of benefit is that of completing the necessary practical tasks, or dealing with first things.

Other activities that often assist with the acknowledgement component include looking through photo albums, reading saved cards and letters, writing thank-you notes for kindnesses demonstrated to you and your family immediately following the death, or the practice of prayer or meditation in which you verbally acknowledge the loss in some way.

Acceptance refers to a process and not a destination. Many times, folks believe that there is some point in the distant future at which they will arrive one day and find themselves in a state of total acceptance of the death of their loved one. This mistaken perception is the foundation for beliefs that falsely promise acceptance after the passage of certain periods of time. For instance, many believe that the one-year anniversary is a magical point in time that should mark complete acceptance of the death. For others, that magical point in time may be six months, while still others hold two years as the destination. The reality is that acceptance is a process at which you will work each day—learning to accept a little more of your changed situation—and not some magical point in time at which we arrive one day.

As you engage life in all of its varied facets, you will progressively move toward a pervasive attitude of acceptance that empowers you to deal more effectively with the whole of your life. The acceptance component becomes a natural byproduct of your daily activities, an outgrowth of your personal determination to stay connected with life and those around you.

Affirmation represents the fuel necessary for successful engagement of the first two components in this choice. As you begin the process of acknowledgement and acceptance, you are likely to find strength by affirming those things that remain. You may start by affirming that you are here and that you possess unique individual strengths and abilities upon which to draw as you face this difficult situation. You can affirm the positive accomplishments in which you may have participated with your loved one, accomplishments such as educational goals, shared hobbies, joint ventures on behalf of charities, children, business development, and so forth.

These joint accomplishments can create a sense of connection with and pride in the relationship. Another area for possible affirmation lies in plans jointly made for the future, such as life insurance plans, annuity programs, and educational provisions. These may help you affirm your ability to move ahead in life despite this devastating blow. Plans made with the future in mind can provide a true sense of connection with and continuity of the relationship.

Through the choice of Acknowledgement, Acceptance, and Affirmation, you begin the process of taking control of those things over which you truly have control—your responses to the events and experiences inherent in life.

The Choice to Mourn the Loss Fully

The second option you face is the choice to Mourn the Loss Fully. It is imperative that this choice receive attention in the Early Mourning Phase because of the way in which our society tends to discourage mourning the loss of a loved one.

Generally, society feels that death is something that can and must be overcome. At the very least, society seeks to minimize death's effects on individuals and groups. For these reasons, our society does not readily encourage or facilitate healthy mourning of personal losses. Obviously, individual support systems vary from one person to another, and you may have a wonderful support system that allows and encourages you to mourn; however, society as a whole does a poor job of permitting you to mourn your loss in healthy ways. In light of this, healthy mourning becomes a personal responsibility.

Grief is a system of emotions and experiences that requires expression rather than repression. Give yourself permission to feel the emotions related to your grief and further express them through healing mourning activities. Repressed or unexpressed grief can have serious detrimental effects on your emotional, mental, physical, and spiritual well-being. As your grief is expressed, it will gradually be drained, leaving healing as its residue.

You can choose to express your grief in many healthy ways, including tears, laughter, quiet contemplation, art, work, play, exercise, talk, touch, writing, reading, prayer, and meditation just to name a few. Once you choose to mourn your loss fully, you will employ a unique combination of mourning activities to create meaning in your life.

As you express your sadness and grief in your own way, be aware that some around you may seek to dictate how you should or should not express your grief. Work to resist those efforts from usually well-meaning individuals and follow your own path to healing. Remember, mourning is an individual process—find healthy ways that work for *you* as you express *your* grief.

The Choice to Embrace the Pain of Mourning

The third choice you face in this Early Mourning Phase is that of embracing the pain of mourning. Once you have entered the acknowledgement/acceptance/affirmation cycle of this phase and have chosen to fully mourn your loss through healthy expression of your feelings and experiences, you are then ready to face this third choice. At some level, you are aware that there can be tremendous pain associated with mourning the loss of a loved one.

I choose the analogy of embracing on purpose. I have never liked partial hugs; give me a good, full, bear-hug embrace anytime! Partial embraces communicate hesitancy, fear, mistrust, disinterest, and any number of other messages that cause us to be tentative in approaching each other. A full embrace—even when there has been a misunderstanding or a difference of opinion—communicates full acceptance and a willingness to work things through. When you choose to embrace the pain of mourning, you are choosing to accept the responsibilities and consequences of your actions as you mourn your loss. A full embrace leaves no lingering questions about what exists in any relationship. The same is true when you embrace the pain of mourning.

Dealing with pain of any sort can be terribly frightening. But choosing to embrace the pain sets the stage for you to move into the next phase of your mourning journey, a phase where you will undertake your most intense grief work. Realize that when you choose to embrace the pain of mourning, you will suffer the anguish that accompanies the loss of a loved one, an experience that cannot be avoided if complete healing is the goal.

This choice involves suffering over a period of time. Good mourning does not happen overnight; it takes time. But the passing of time, in and of itself, does not create healing. The key to healing lies in what you choose to do with the time you have. Both the process of mourning and time are commodities that must be invested in order to affect your life in healthy ways. When you choose to suffer and endure the pain of mourning over the long haul, you will have chosen the path to healthy reconciliation of your grief.

Efforts to avoid the pain of mourning can only bring with them the potential for even greater pain in the future. I encourage you to be realistic about this embrace. You are embracing the pain of mourning and you *will* suffer, yet as you endure this suffering, healthy reconciliation of your grief can produce positive results for you and your family.

The power of choice enables you to start the process of regaining a sense of control over your life following loss. The choices associated with the Early Morning Phase of the grief process set the stage for a successful and meaningful journey. The three choices unique to this phase are as follows:

- **The Choice of Acknowledgement, Acceptance and Affirmation**

- **The Choice to Mourn the Loss Fully**

- **The Choice to Embrace the Pain of Mourning**

~~~

"Of course I will!"

What the hell have I just done? I recall thinking after responding to the principal of Christy's school on Tuesday evening. After informing me that the school was holding a memorial service on the morning of the funeral, he asked if I would like to speak. "Of course I will," I had responded. *What was I thinking? I know, I WASN'T thinking! I was tempted to call and decline the offer . . . but I felt compelled to speak. What would I do? What would I say?*

I knew how difficult it had been for me to go to the wrecking yard earlier in the day to see the car. I only made it within fifty feet of the car before turning back. I just couldn't do it! As I sat contemplating my agreement to speak at the school's service, I had a thought. I would return to the wrecking yard the next day to see if a second trip would be easier. My thought was that if making an initial trip to a place made the second one easier, then perhaps it would work for the school as well.

Wednesday dawned, and I drove to the wrecking yard. Sure enough, my trip the day before had presented me with the opportunity to absorb the initial onslaught of feelings associated with the situation. During that second trip, I was able to examine the car in complete detail. I was emotional at times but not debilitated by my intense feelings of grief. Late that afternoon, I drove to Plano East Senior High School and just walked the campus. I allowed myself to experience all the emotions associated with that stroll. Internally assured that the next day would be a little easier, I left feeling confident that I would be able to address the students and faculty appropriately.

~~~

"Have you ever thought about teaching?" I recall my father-in-law asking as we left campus following the memorial service.

I had indeed thought about teaching but was curious about what prompted his question, so I asked him to explain.

"Well, you just seemed so natural and comfortable in there addressing the student body and teachers. I think you would be good," he responded.

I did not immediately share with him my little experiment. I merely thanked him and acknowledged that I had indeed considered becoming a teacher.

What grew from that experience was awareness that I would have to proactively address all of the issues related to my personal loss. I discovered that going through the grief process was going to be painful and that I would have to work every day to embrace the tasks associated with healthy grief work. I also discovered that my family members were not the only ones deeply affected by Christy's death. Her students, colleagues, and countless others were touched as well. I owed it to everyone involved to be as healthy as I could. I began therapy within two weeks.

~~~

Questions for Reflection

- What possibilities come to mind as you contemplate the power of choice?

- Looking back at your life, what kinds of activities have helped you most as you have dealt with other losses?

- Based on the answers to the previous question, how can you see yourself using those same activities as you mourn this loss?

- A popular phrase is: "Time heals!" In light of the information contained in this section, what is your response to that statement?

Mid-Mourning—The Transition

Once you have negotiated the difficult first days of the funeral and handled the details discussed in Appendix A of this book, you will enter into the Mid-Mourning or Transition Phase of the mourning process. This phase may be characterized by the intense grief work that comes into play. The importance of this phase cannot be emphasized enough—for the way in which you move through this phase can have a tremendous effect on how you continue on with your life.

If you choose to ignore issues or submerge the feelings associated with the Mid-Mourning transition period, it is likely that your continuation in life will be colored by these choices in negative ways.

If, on the other hand, you choose to engage in healthy grief work in this transition phase, you may be able to move along with your life in much more healthy and positive ways. Obviously, the choice is yours.

This section will provide a framework to help you examine your options as you continue to deal with your loss.

The Characteristics of Mid-Mourning

As the cards, letters, and calls become less frequent and the lives of those who were there for you early on begin to get back to normal, yours will not. You will find yourself faced with the harsh reality of the loss you have suffered.

Often, people will mistakenly believe that the most difficult time in a loss situation comes immediately after the loss and will respond in kind. But this is not often true. Typically, the time you need support the most will be the time it is least available.

You may find yourself facing much of this time alone as you work to find some semblance of order and normalcy. It is important to understand some of the major characteristics and situations you will face in this transition. Again, emotions and situations mentioned here may be experienced in any of phases, but they typically characterize this middle phase.

Knowing up front that most people who supported me and my family right after the death of my husband would essentially disappear when I needed support the most, helped me make plans to ask for support during the time of transition.

"Debbie" (age 38)

Deep Separation Pain and/or Anxiety

As the reality of your loss begins to sink in, you may experience a deep separation pain. You realize that the person you lost will never return to you physically. A deep sense of yearning for the person may set in as well as a longing for things to be as they were before the loss. Sometimes this yearning and longing can become so intense that you may try to bargain with God, the stars, or some other higher power to make things as they were before. This wishing or bargaining is also prevalent in anticipatory grief — as when a loved one endures an extended illness prior to succumbing in death. It is important to understand that while these feelings are a perfectly no**rmal part of grieving, they are still a form of magical thinking and cannot alter reality in any way.**

The anxiety associated with separation from your loved one can vary in intensity and duration. Anxiety may be mild and infrequent one day and extreme and persistent the next. It may be situational and associated with routines in which you engaged with your loved one. Attending social or religious meetings, going to the grocery store, shopping at the mall, taking a stroll in the park, eating at a favorite restaurant, or watching a favorite television program are all examples of situations in which you might experience a sense of anxiety. These experiences are common and are not a sign that you are losing it. Instead of allowing this free-floating anxiety to dominate your thoughts and actions, work instead to use the experiences to reflect on and remember your loved one, acknowledge and affirm the uniqueness of your relationship.

Sometimes the experience of anxiety can blossom into a full-blown, activity-arresting panic attack. If you find yourself in this situation, seek out a safe place to sit down and concentrate on taking deep breaths, using your diaphragm to regulate the pace of your breathing, and focus on thoughts that are calming and connect you with something tangible. If the experiences of anxiety continue at a severe level, get help from a medical or mental health professional. They can provide support that will help you cope with these extreme experiences of anxiety.

Difficulty Distinguishing Fact from Fantasy

In addition to the separation pain and anxiety can come a need to identify with your loved one to the point that you may have trouble distinguishing fact from **fantasy. D**reams involving the deceased, hallucinations of seeing the deceased in familiar settings, or imagining that you hear them walking or speaking occur routinely in some instances. These experiences often appear very real and at times can be rather unsettling. Please know that these happenings are common to many and are not an indication that you are losing touch with reality. It is not surprising that you may become confused at times as you work to sort through the emotions you are facing. Everything may seem to be in a state of disarray. Allow yourself to experience these situations as they occur and work to not ignore or repress them. Share these experiences with a trusted friend or counselor. In doing so, you will enable yourself to move along in the process in a healthy manner.

When I realized that I was not going crazy — that others experienced the same kinds of things as I did — I felt much more at ease talking about my grief!

"Robert" (age 50)

Physical Symptoms

It is likely that you may experience various physical symptoms connected with your process of grief. Sleep disturbances, altered appetite, anxiety attacks, headaches, stomach aches, tightness in the chest, and shortness of breath are common physical symptoms experienced by those in this phase of the mourning process. You may also be more susceptible to illness since you are likely to be exhausted at times and your immune system weakened. It is advisable to contact your family physician as soon as possible for assistance in monitoring your health. The support your physician provides is invaluable as you work to reconcile yourself to this loss. Not only can your doctor objectively evaluate your physical health, he or she may also be able to point you toward additional resources of support as well.

Flooding of Emotions

As the reality of your loss continues to sink in, you are likely to experience a flood of emotions—many times, more intensely than you ever have before. Occasionally, it may be difficult to distinguish one emotion from another since they are all battling for attention and expression at the same time. It may feel like the dam has broken and you are in danger of drowning in the flood. Repressing these emotions can be unhealthy, but working to feel and express them as they surface can cause the flooding to abate sometimes. One way to do this is to say something like, *"Right now I am feeling mixed up! I feel angry and sad and alone all at once!"* The ability to label emotions can at least provide you with some semblance of order in what otherwise can become chaotic confusion. As you begin to identify and separate individual emotions from within the deluge, you are likely to feel less overwhelmed in the process.

Intense Sadness and Loneliness

Feelings of intense sadness and loneliness are likely to occur as the reality of the loss drives itself into your consciousness. These emotions can be overwhelming at times and may cause you to feel completely helpless and lost. You may find yourself struggling between the decision to be around people or seek solitude when you feel lonely and sad. Even in the presence of others, you may still experience a sense of loneliness. For this reason, you may often find yourself choosing to avoid gatherings of any size. "What good is it if I still feel lonely when I am with others?" is a question often asked by people in your situation.

At times, you may feel like you have to mask your sadness when you are around others and pretend that everything is fine. I encourage you instead to risk being with people and allow yourself to express your sadness in their presence. Both you and those around you may benefit from these expressions of feeling. You may find release, and they may learn to be more at ease around you. Seeking to be with people when you are feeling sad and lonely can be a gift to them and to you, helping ease the pain of all those going through this phase.

Guilt Feelings

Guilt is another emotion common to the Mid-Mourning Phase of grief. You may find yourself feeling guilty about being the one left behind or about not doing enough to show your love for the deceased before he or she died. You may also feel guilty about having received an inheritance or insurance settlement following the death. And you may feel guilty about not being able to follow through on promises you made to your loved one.

Guilt can come from the mistaken belief that the death of your loved one is some sort of punishment for something you either did or failed to do; it may also come because of past fleeting thoughts or wishes that your loved one would die — yet another example of how magical thinking can exert influence on your experiences of grief. Guilt can come because of a perception that you have done something terrible, stupid, or inappropriate following the death of your loved one.

You may be able to convince yourself to feel guilty about almost anything connected with the death of your loved one, regardless of how illogical the thought or situation might be. Guilt can be either real or false. Genuine guilt comes because of some inappropriate action or word that requires forgiveness. False guilt, on the other hand, surfaces with almost no explanation or reason. Often, the guilt felt by survivors is false and is a learned behavior or habit. You would be wise to talk with someone who understands this guilt phenomenon and can help you challenge those illogical guilt thoughts and feelings. Realize that if you feel guilty in any way connected with the death of your loved one, you need to take steps to talk these thoughts and feelings through with someone who cares and understands.

Guilt feelings are common in the aftermath of a death, but not all guilt is justified. Work to determine the kind of guilt you are experiencing and then deal with it appropriately.

Feelings of Depression

Often, you may feel depressed as the reality becomes more apparent in your daily life. Depression is another common response to your loss. Many days you may feel like staying in bed and not going anywhere or doing anything with anyone. When you feel depressed, you may experience a decrease in physical energy and a lack of interest in activities you normally enjoy. Mourning takes a tremendous amount of energy, and you may feel completely drained from time to time.

As you work through your mourning, you may feel weak, disinterested, or experience a heavy feeling in your chest. Crying often and unexpectedly is common as well, **and** you may experience a sense of emptiness from time to time. Your thoughts may center on the uselessness of life and living or your perceived unworthiness as a person. All these experiences are a part of the normal feelings of depression associated with a death loss. Although you may believe that these feelings will go on forever, they will pass. You are not having a breakdown, and your feelings do not indicate weakness on your part. This depression is part of what you need in order to say goodbye to your loved one.

One word of caution is in order, however. If you begin experiencing chronic depression and you cannot seem to pull yourself out of it through mourning activities such as talking, exercise, or writing, you may need to visit with a medical or mental health professional. Remember that you must take care of yourself to move successfully through the grief process.

Feelings of Powerlessness, Abandonment, and Victimization Resulting in Anger and Rage

Anger and rage are also common responses to loss. As the reality of your loss becomes more apparent in your life, the anger and rage you may feel can deepen and intensify. You may direct your anger at any number of targets. You may experience feelings of anger toward the person who died. You may feel anger toward God for either taking your loved one away from you or for not doing anything to keep him or her alive. You may find yourself feeling anger toward a doctor or another medical practitioner connected with the care of your loved one. You may even find yourself feeling anger toward people not connected to the death in any way, or you might discover that you are angry with yourself for something you perceive that you could or should have done before your loved one died.

Your anger may turn into a type of rage as you seek to find someone or something to blame for the death. You might find yourself wanting to strike out verbally or physically. Many times, in an effort to deal with the potentially intense feelings of anger and rage, you may displace your anger by expressing it toward someone or something not related to your loss in any way.

To a great degree, this anger stems from feeling powerless, abandoned, and victimized. Feeling God, the world, all the forces of the universe have teamed up against you and taken a precious person from your life will naturally incite anger.

Many times people think that simply expressing anger and rage in random and unfocused ways is the only option available to them. But frequently, these random expressions only compound the feelings of powerlessness and victimization.

Expressing your feelings verbally and physically is perfectly acceptable—as long as you do not present a potential harm to yourself, others, or property in the venting. As an alternative to randomly venting your anger, you may find some relief by taking constructive action instead.

My experience with mourners tells me that many have found release through physical activities such as walking, running, lifting weights, chopping wood, gardening, and the like. I have also seen folks release the energy of anger by hitting a punching bag, slamming a tennis racket on a mattress, hitting golf balls at the driving range, or visiting the batting cage. Once the physical energy associated with anger has dissipated, mourners are more likely to find the perspective to deal constructively with their anger.

You may find relief by channeling your anger into actions to improve a situation connected with the death of your loved one. Working to raise community awareness in some positive way may provide you with an avenue in which to purposefully express your anger. Consider establishing a support group for individuals in situations similar to yours, requesting that educational resources be made available to individuals in similar situations, establishing a scholarship fund in memory of your loved one, or undertaking other such endeavors.

Remember that there are also dangers in over involvement in causes. Activity is good as long as you do not allow it to mask or substitute your true feelings. It is crucial to face your feelings while engaging in constructive expressions of those emotions. This blending of feeling and expression can help you mourn your loss more completely.

Feelings of anger and rage are to be expected. You are encouraged to express that anger and rage in appropriate and helpful ways. As you express those emotions, you will drain them, thereby opening the pathways for reconciliation and recovery. In constructively expressing anger, you will also begin regaining a sense of control over your life—control that will empower you to fight the feelings of helplessness and victimization more effectively.

Feelings of Fear and Panic

A final pair of emotions characteristic of the Mid-Mourning Phase is fear and panic. At times, you may be faced with an overwhelming sense of fear that something dreadful is about to happen to you or someone you love. This sense of fear and panic can produce some very real physical, mental, and emotional symptoms. Realize that you have real reasons for feeling this way. You have come face-to-face with the most devastating of all human experiences—the death of a loved one.

You may feel extremely vulnerable and weak. You may feel the need to lock yourself away from the world and its potential dangers. Again, these are normal feelings during this intense phase of grief. Seek ways to express them constructively, but work to avoid giving in to the feelings of fear and panic. Giving in to them often brings on a type of emotional and relational paralysis that can grow.

Fears are often the result of an overactive imagination fueled by the death of your loved one. One acronym I have read describes F.E.A.R. as Fictitious Events Appearing Real. Talking about your fears with someone routinely opens the door for you to examine them in more detail. Sharing them with a caring sounding board provides a different perspective and can help reframe the fears you are feeling.

One important question I use frequently when faced with fears is: "What proof do I have that what I fear will actually take place?" Fears often have their genesis in illogical trains of thought. Seeking proof often helps distinguish between the legitimate and trumped-up concerns associated with the experience of fear.

Panic is a natural outgrowth of unchecked fear. When faced with a situation that normally creates the fight-or-flight response, you might find yourself in a freeze mode, unable to move, think, decide, or act. If you ever find yourself in this situation, find a place to sit down; focus on your breathing, slow down, clear your mind, and walk yourself backwards through the sequence of events that just occurred. Once you have found the beginning point, focus on the "What proof do I have that . . ." question in order to put what happened into a perspective grounded in the present moment. As always, if feelings of fear and panic increase or you find yourself unable to manage them well, visiting with a professional counselor or therapist might be in order.

The Transition or Mid-Mourning Phase of the grief process is perhaps the most crucial of all three phases. The Mid-Mourning Phase is the one in which you will conduct the lion's share of your grief work, and it is the one that will most likely have the greatest effect on your ability to continue building a healthy new life. In keeping with this reality, the feelings and experiences characteristic of this phase are equally weighty. Understanding these feelings and experiences can set the stage for more uniform and focused grief work. The characteristics of this phase are:

- **Deep Separation Pain and/or Anxiety**

- **Difficulty Distinguishing Fact from Fantasy**

- **Physical Symptoms**

- **Flooding of Emotions**

- **Intense Sadness and Loneliness**

- **Guilt Feelings**

- **Feelings of Depression**

- **Feelings of Powerlessness, Abandonment, and Victimization Resulting in Anger and Rage**

- **Feelings of Fear and Panic**

"You want me to do WHAT?" At first, I thought he was kidding when my therapist suggested that I go to the telephone pole Christy had hit. He said I should take an aluminum baseball bat and hit the pole as a way to tap and release my anger. He wasn't kidding, and I was intrigued. You can imagine how foolish I felt pulling off the side of the road, getting out of the car, taking my baseball bat, positioning myself beside the pole, and then beating the heck out of it—right there in front of God and everybody! People slowed to stare at this madman assaulting a telephone pole, but once I got started, it felt good, and I completely lost myself in the task.

I quickly realized that in order for me to move through the mourning process in healthy ways, I would have to actively embrace all the related feelings and experiences. During those first few months of therapy, I felt such intense emotions, experienced such diverse thoughts, and was more ill physically than ever before. I was hit with everything imaginable and then some. Through it all, however, I realized that only by engaging my grief proactively would I ever have hope of healing. It was a lesson of lasting importance.

~~~

Questions for Reflection

- After reading this section, what set of experiences or emotions presents the biggest challenge for you?

- What set of emotions or experiences are you most comfortable dealing with?

- Does knowing that the emotions and experiences discussed are common make a difference for you? If so, in what ways?

The Challenges of Mid-Mourning

Perhaps the best way to describe the Mid-Mourning Phase is that it is a period of working out your grief. The picture that comes to my mind is one of a gym equipped with weight machines, free weights, stationary bicycles, stair-step machines, treadmills, mirrors, and scales. I envision a person entering the gym and determining exactly which equipment to use for that particular day's workout. The person realizes that the workout will require effort and that a certain amount of time will be involved. The person also realizes that in order for the workouts to be useful or produce the intended outcome, they must be conducted on a consistent basis. The idea of getting into shape through working out carries the concepts of involvement, effort, patience, time, fatigue, frustration, and ultimately, accomplishment. The physical, emotional, mental, and spiritual benefits of exercise are widely known.

In like manner, going through a time of working out your grief can bring about the same benefits as physical exercise, only applied to your emotional and relational well-being. The Mid-Mourning or Transition Phase of grief also includes effort, involvement, patience, time, fatigue, frustration, and ultimately, accomplishment.

Can you imagine going into a gym dressed to work out, then just sitting and looking at the machines, asking them to get you in shape without putting forth any effort? Neither can I! That would seem ridiculous, wouldn't it? Yet, many people enter this phase of the process with that kind of attitude, looking for an easier way through, a quick fix or way to bypass it altogether. This is the most difficult part of the entire process, and it's the part that demands the most from you!

It would be great if you could just skip this part and move on to the final phase. The only problem is that for you to continue with your life in a healthy, integrated manner, you must go through the workout part of the process. Otherwise, you run the risk of carrying unreconciled grief issues with you, potentially adversely affecting your relationships and responsibilities in the future.

In keeping with this workout theme, you will face four specific challenges in this Mid-Mourning Phase of grief. In the same way that you work out different muscle groups in the gym, you will tackle each of these challenges individually as part of your total grief workout. These workout challenges can be defined as: Adjusting Your Perspective and Investment, Checking Your Reality, Finding Stability, and Structuring Your Grief.

How long will these visits to the grief gym last before you are ready to move on to the next phase? This is something I can't define, since the mourning experience is as unique as each individual is. Some have indicated that it takes from two to four years to fully mourn the death of a loved one, provided active engagement takes place. This intense period of grief and mourning is neither completely predictable nor determined by specific periods of time. Many factors and variables can affect your progress. Yet, with healthy grief work or mourning, you may begin experiencing a noticeable difference and healing between six months and a year following your loss.

By employing healthy mourning strategies, you may begin to see and feel the changes necessary for moving on with your life. As you work through the four areas of grief workouts, you will be making the transitions necessary to continue in a healthy manner, mentally, emotionally, physically, and spiritually.

Adjusting Your Perspective and Investment

The first challenge of this phase requires Adjusting Your Perspective and Investment — essentially, shifting the focus of the relationship from one of active participation to one of access and memory. This does not mean disconnecting from the emotions surrounding the loss; those must be dealt with and expressed. What this does mean is working on the reality that your loved one has indeed died and that you will not have the privilege of seeing or being with that person physically again. It means that you must begin the process of acknowledging that you can no longer actively invest physical, emotional, mental, or spiritual energy into a relationship that only exists in memory. It means that you must begin the process of learning to live off the interest of that relationship by using your energy to re-invest in other active relationships — relationships with yourself, other family members, friends, and those in your yet-to-be-determined future.

This can be a very difficult challenge to face simply because you have a history, a pattern of relating to your loved one that has been established over time. As you go through the experience of grieving and mourning the death of your loved one, you are likely to discover many life lessons that hold merit as you work to reconcile yourself to this change and build a new life as a result. As those life lessons are discovered, rediscovered, or affirmed, you will find yourself with many opportunities to reinvest in other existing or new relationships. This possibility is one of the beautiful aspects of mourning—we can actually extend the influence of that relationship that now exists only in memory into the fabric of current relationships, knowing that as we do so, the ripple effect of such reinvestments will continue long after we ourselves are gone. This process is a way of perpetuating the influence of our loved one to a larger world.

Checking Your Reality

The second challenge that must be encountered is that of checking your reality. This challenge involves monitoring your personal efforts to distinguish between the loss event that has occurred and your responses to it. In a sense, it is an extension of the first challenge of Adjusting Your Perspective and Investment. As you work to reallocate emotional energy from the lost relationship elsewhere, you will need a way to check the nature of the reality in which you are now living. These checks are likely to occur through two distinct, yet related activities: reviewing and sorting through the relationship.

Living in the reality of "here and now" demands that we review the relationship we had with our loved one. The relationship has obviously changed to one of memory rather than activity. It is no longer growing and dynamic. It is held captive in thought, pictures, words, perceptions, and experiences, all of which are accessible for review and reflection.

Realize that in addition to the positive aspects of the relationship, the review process may uncover areas that might also be somewhat painful. People are not perfect, and therefore, relationships are not perfect either. You are likely to go back to the very beginning of your relationship and review each aspect and each event, evaluating the significance and value each holds for you. You will review things said or not said; things completed or left unfinished; and dreams, hopes, and plans that were realized or unfulfilled.

You may also recognize that there were things about the person or relationship you were not particularly fond of. These unpleasant memories may also surface in the review process. The importance of conducting the relationship review lies in being able to sharpen the clarity of the relationship: what it meant and still means to you; what things were useful and what things were hindering; which areas were fulfilling and which areas were stifling; which areas produced regret, guilt, and suffering; and which produced pride, comfort, and strength.

It is not uncommon for a survivor to place the lost loved one and the relationship they shared on a pedestal of perfection that cannot be compared or replaced. Since perfection does not exist, it is imperative that you look honestly at both the person and the relationship in order to gain a clear picture of the reality in which you now find yourself. Once you have constructed a clear, realistic picture of the relationship, you may find yourself better able to distinguish the useful from the useless, the exciting from the mundane, the enriching from the discounting, the warm from the cold, and the happy from the sad—all of which are parts of every significant relationship. This picture will help you tackle the second part of the grief workout—Checking Your Reality—as you sort through the relationship.

In reviewing, you list the good, bad, and indifferent—every aspect of your relationship with your loved one. You look at each in a broad sense but don't assign a weight or importance of one aspect over another. In the next step, sorting through the relationship, you take the information retrieved in the review process and sort through the various aspects you uncovered. This part is a more specific; it is a little like separating your clothes on washday.

To keep clothes looking their best, you separate the whites from the colors, the permanent press from the delicate, and the hand washables from the clothes to be dry cleaned or professionally laundered. Throwing all of your clothing together and treating them the same on washday will produce disastrous results. The same can be true if you fail to sort through your memories. Not all memories carry the same weight, and not all memories and experiences need the same amount or type of attention. As you sort through your memories and experiences, you will begin measuring and assigning importance to each. Analysis and careful examination are important to this process.

At this point, your real grief begins to take shape and form. You will probably want to continue to carry the best parts of the relationship and its influences with you after this loss. You may also discover that you will be able to uncover mistakes made in the relationship and learn valuable lessons that can be carried with you as you progress through your grief. Sorting through the relationship can help you determine areas of your lifestyle and relationship patterns that need to be changed, discarded, or eliminated to help ensure healthy reconciliation and continuation.

Through the total process of reviewing and sorting, you will examine pleasant memories, painful memories, aspects of the relationship with your loved one that you will always save, and aspects that are best let go. Remember that all experiences can affect you both positively and negatively; you must decide for yourself how much each memory or experience will affect your life from now on. In the challenge of Checking Your Reality, you review your relationship, sort through the experiences, and select which influences you will carry with you as you continue your journey.

Finding Stability

The third challenge of the Mid-Mourning Phase is that of Finding Stability. The Mid-Mourning Phase brings a tremendous amount of disorganization and confusion. Nothing is the same as it was before the loss event. You may feel differently about yourself, your status, your family, your relationships, your roles—everything has changed!

You may perceive that people treat you differently than before, and in many cases, you will be correct. They may try to smother you with attention and advice, or you may feel abandoned by them. As strange as it may seem, both may be true. Often people will go to both extremes as they attempt to deal with either their discomfort about death and mortality or their ambivalent feelings toward you. In either case, their responses and actions can contribute to your sense of disorganization and confusion. In light of this, the need for a sense of stability may become more acute.

Finding stability will require restructuring all of your relationships from the perspective of one untouched by loss to that of one changed by the death of a loved one. This challenge may be compounded by others who are dependent on you in some way—a spouse, children, grandchildren, siblings, or other family members—who are also experiencing their own grief and may look to you for strength, guidance and support.

Because your most intense grief work will be conducted during this phase, much of your energy will be focused on you. The presence of other dependents requires that you also focus some of that energy on them; however, you must realize that finding stability for yourself will ultimately provide an atmosphere or model of stability for those dependent on you. This realization may help you feel better about directing attention toward yourself so you can focus better on the needs of those dependents. This concept finds validity in preflight protocol when passengers are instructed, in the event of loss of cabin pressure, to place the mask over their own faces before assisting children with theirs. You will be unable to assist others if you are incapacitated. Remember, creating stability for yourself forms the foundation for others who depend on you to find their own ways of healing.

You are different now than you were before the loss of your loved one. You will never be the same, and neither will those close to you and your family. The challenge of finding stability means that you must face the differences within yourself, your family, and your world in realistic terms. To find stability, you may need to learn new approaches to decision making and problem solving, discover different areas from which to draw support, and explore meaningful new ways to relate to the world around you.

The challenge of finding stability requires you to face yourself in ways you may never have before. This challenge to begin rebuilding a new life is not unlike the challenge faced by those whose property, belongings, and work have been destroyed by a natural disaster. Experiencing the death of a loved one is much like surviving the devastation of an earthquake, the terror of a hurricane, or the fury of a tornado. You are left to start over, and you must begin by finding stability for the grueling tasks ahead.

Structuring Your Grief

The fourth challenge you will face in the Mid-Mourning Phase is that of Structuring Your Grief. The grief experience cannot be wrapped in a neat package. It doesn't come complete with instructions and guarantees, thoroughly predictable and contained. Although the grief process is identifiable, defined, or traceable, it is not something that can be passed through quickly or with minimal effort. There are no shortcuts or magical formulas to make your journey easier.

Structuring your grief can be very much like the process of making a pot on a potter's wheel. A good therapist friend of mine introduced me to the concept of "Green Grief" one day as we visited together. He explained that as we mourn the loss of a loved one, we begin to mold or structure our grieving into something we can be comfortable with. We begin to make sense of our lives and mourn our loss in ways that are meaningful to us personally. As we meet the challenges of this particular phase, we open doors to creating a new person through the process.

A rough pot, vase, bowl, or platter has the familiar form of the intended final product, yet is still very fragile and soft, subject to the possibility of falling apart, until it has been fired. In this stage of creation, when it has yet to reach completion or maturity through the final firing process, it is called greenware. Many times, the artist must make adjustments in his or her creation due to impurities in the clay or asymmetry problems before the final firing of the work of art.

Your work of grief and mourning during this phase is very much the same. You are beginning to form a new you as you grieve and mourn. You are looking honestly at your relationship with your loved one as well as your relationship with yourself and others. You are beginning the exploration process of what it is you want to do and become. You are structuring a rough new you. You are likely to be very fragile and make some mistakes along the way. You may find yourself making alterations and adjustments to what it is you want to become; you may even have to start over in certain areas from time to time. Much like pottery in the green ware stage, you are in the "green grief" part of your work; you are learning about yourself in ways you may never have before. You are preparing for the final firing process.

The Mid-Mourning transition phase provides you with the opportunity to work on new and different approaches in discovering who you are and shows you how to best express those discoveries. Be gentle with yourself when you make mistakes. Open the door to experience all the emotions of this particular phase. Give yourself permission to change your mind and grow. Do not be afraid to experience solitude, for it is in solitude that much of your creative work will be accomplished.

The challenge is structuring your grief. The reward is self-knowledge. The outcome is the opportunity to move ahead to the next set of challenges with confidence.

The Mid-Mourning Phase of the grief process may be likened to a series of workouts in a gym. When a person commits to a gym membership and establishes goals associated with his or her participation, the logical conclusion is that the person will work consistently toward those goals by participating in regular workout sessions. Committing to working out your grief in the Mid-Mourning Phase will provide the framework for healing. The four challenges of grief workouts in this phase are:

- **Adjusting Your Perspective and Investment**

- **Checking Your Reality**

  o **Conducting a Relationship Review, and**

  o **Sorting through Your Relationship**

- **Finding Stability**

- **Structuring Your Grief**

"Talkin's the shots!" Yes, talkin's the shots! Kacie got it . . . in the same way I had. Learning to live without Christy required talking about our thoughts, feelings, and experiences, regardless of the difficulty. That statement came in response to a question I asked her at the end of a story I made up in an effort to encourage her to share her feelings.

It seems that she had not been feeling well; she'd had stomachaches, headaches, and general listlessness for about two weeks. I noticed that the onset of this change in her health coincided with a drastic drop in talking about Christy on her part. I told her a story about a man who was sick on the inside and how he went to the doctor for help. After checking him out, the doctor confirmed that the man was indeed sick. The man became angry. He knew he was sick! He wanted to know how to get well!

The doctor informed him that he could get well by taking a long series of shots. The man was not interested in the least and told the doctor so. He did not like shots; hated pain; cringed at the sight of blood. There had to be an easier way, a pill he could take, something! The doctor told the man that there were no shortcuts to his healing; however, he had a choice. He could either take the long series of shots, endure the small pain, and ultimately get well, or refuse the shots and live with the larger pain inside from that point on. After contemplating a moment, he decided to take the shots.

Following that story, I looked at Kacie—a seven year-old, mind you—and asked her, "Kacie, how are you and that sick man alike?"

She sat for a moment, folded her arms across her chest, stuck out her bottom lip, cut her eyes at me, and said, "Talkin's the shots, Daddy! Talkin's the shots!"

Talking helped, whether it came in the form of visiting with another friend, running, engaging in weekly therapy, writing in my journal, running, reading books on grief, spending time with friends, running, allowing tears to flow freely, visiting places both Christy and I loved, running . . . you get the idea. I found multiple ways to "take my shots." Oh, did I mention I did a lot of running?

~~~

I remember the day I bought my ticket to wellness. Up until that day, I had no real label for my intents and purposes as I moved through my time of transition. I knew that life was different and that I was different as well; I just wasn't sure about how to take control of what I would ultimately become. About five months after her death, I bought *The Seven Habits of Highly Effective People*, by Stephen Covey. In that book, he has a chapter entitled "Begin with the End in Mind." For me, beginning with **the end in mind meant** envisioning my life as one filled with purpose, peace, and power. It focused my efforts on a goal. It created a framework in which to conduct all the necessary work of mourning ahead of me. I realized that day that if I wanted to arrive at my intended destination, I would have to take a journey, paying attention to everything around me in the process. I bought my ticket to wellness!

~~~

The challenges inherent in that time of transition forced me to look inside in ways I never had before. They caused me to ask questions of myself I had never conceived. They took me to places that required my attention. They opened the doors to possibilities I never knew existed. They established the framework in which I began to discover my personal potential. They revealed the powerful truth that if I were to ever heal, I had to mourn well because "talkin's the shots!"

Questions for Reflection

- When thinking about living off the interest of the relationship you had with your departed loved one, what three lessons come to mind that you anticipate being able to reinvest into other relationships?

- Set aside some time to conduct your relationship review, listing all areas of your relationship that come to mind. Once that is complete, begin sorting through those areas and assigning weight and meaning to them as explained in the section on Checking Your Reality. This process may take more than one session, which is perfectly fine. Take as much time as you need.

- In what areas do you find the most need for stability? What actions have you taken in the past that have helped create stability that you could employ now?

The Choices of Mid-Mourning

The Choices of the Mid-Mourning Phase flow naturally from the challenges of the transition period. In this phase, you will have the opportunity to consider three choices as you continue your process of good mourning. Your choices are to Be Alone, Assert Yourself, and Begin Rebuilding. Each choice goes hand-in-hand with the intense grief work associated with this phase. Again, the transition period is crucial to your ability to move ahead with your life in healthy and useful ways. At first, you may find yourself exploring these choices tentatively, feeling a bit unsure of yourself. This is perfectly natural and you need not feel discouraged if you find yourself struggling with them at times. As with any new activity or skill, the more you practice, the better you become.

The Choice to Be Alone

The choice to Be Alone is one of the most difficult you will ever have to make in the process of mourning. There is something quite fearful in realizing that grief work is very personal and that you are responsible for your own progress. Yet, in order to face the challenges of Mid-Mourning mentioned earlier, you *must* choose to be alone from time to time. This is a choice of courage, a choice that indicates your readiness to face the real tasks of getting on with your life.

You are likely to find yourself alone with your thoughts, feelings, and responses periodically. It is a choice to stop the over pursuit of activities which may have previously kept you from looking honestly at your situation. Burying yourself in busyness is a common reaction to loss situations. Activities related to work, church involvement, diverse social functions, and those that call upon you to take care of other, usually weaker individuals are all noble endeavors. And at first glance, many of these activities carry varying degrees of merit. Yet the over pursuit of these activities may become a barrier to healthy grief work. Over participation in these activities may be attempts to forget or push aside what has happened to you.

Additionally, there are dangers in becoming overly involved in activities that promise to medicate or dull of the pain you are experiencing. Be aware that you may be tempted to medicate feelings of pain, loneliness, and despair through drug or alcohol use or abuse as well as promiscuous sexual behaviors. Excessive participation in illogical religious rituals, frenetic unfocused activity, or partying can also represent attempts to avoid the pain associated with mourning. Pain in and of itself is not bad or harmful. Pain can be indicating an area that needs attention. It is extremely difficult to deal with something that needs attention if you have dulled your senses to that pain.

The choice to Be Alone is a choice to deal realistically with your loss as well as the accompanying pain. It is a time to examine the meanings this loss has in your life, a time to evaluate whether you are merely reacting to the loss or consciously responding to it. It is a time to begin taking stock of what you have, who you are, and how you intend to use those discoveries in your future actions and plans.

By choosing to be alone, you have the chance to gain important insights into yourself and the world around you as well as your relationships with others. It enables you to begin your wisdom search as you mourn, wisdom so very necessary as you rebuild your life following this loss.

You must realize that the choice to Be Alone requires that you occasionally isolate yourself from friends and family. You will need time alone in order to conduct your relationship review and sort through your experiences with your loved one and to determine how this entire process has affected you.

The solitude of being alone is more than just a spatial experience. It encompasses an attitude as well. Often, you may find yourself among people and still choose to be introspective—thinking about aspects of your relationship or memories that surface when triggered by a particular conversation or activity. This too is the choice to Be Alone, alone with your thoughts and feelings, even in the presence of others.

This choice to Be Alone and isolate yourself *can* cause some trepidation as well. *What if those around me forget that I exist or need company? What if they stop including me in their activities because I appear to be doing just fine? What will I do when I need to talk with someone about my thoughts or discoveries and no one is close by?*

Obviously, the choice to Be Alone does not mean that you totally shut yourself away from friends and family. On the contrary, you should seek a sort of balance between your alone time and your time with others. You will need people who can serve as sounding boards for some of your thoughts and discoveries. The process of being alone can enable you to be more open to suggestions, books, support group participation, counseling, or other relaxing and therapeutic activities that other survivors have found beneficial in similar circumstances.

The beauty of the choice to Be Alone lies in the personal discoveries, explorations, questions, and alternatives that will evolve as you progress. Books, movies, lectures, plays, and discussions with friends can all become springboards for evaluation, reevaluation, change, and discovery.

Again, the choice to Be Alone is a choice of courage. It takes courage to look honestly at yourself, the relationship with your deceased loved one, your responses to the loss, and where you think you might want to go from here. It is the choice to work at balancing alone time and people time—both of which are necessary when you choose to Be Alone.

The Choice to Assert Yourself

The second choice of the Mid-Mourning Phase is the choice to Assert Yourself. Asserting yourself means taking a stand, making a positive statement, or making a declaration. This too is a choice of courage because these assertions are often made in the face of some degree of opposition, from either yourself or others around you.

You are a different person now. Just how different you are and will become are directly related to the discoveries you make about yourself in your alone times. In choosing to assert yourself, you must take all the information revealed in those times of reflection and decide who you are, what you want to become, and how you plan to accomplish these tasks. These decisions will be made known in the form of life assertions. In making life assertions, you decide to take responsibility for yourself, your actions, and your future. This entire process may be encapsulated in the word "change."

The process of asserting yourself begins with a change in your thinking, which ultimately emerges in positive actions. In the very beginning of the mourning process, you may feel unable to go on with your life. Feelings of despair, loneliness, and longing tend to reinforce these thoughts. During the process of evaluation, however, you uncover a tremendous amount of information about yourself, your relationship, and your world. This is all accomplished on a day-to-day basis.

After a period of discovery, you may realize that you have been living and growing and making decisions, maybe even doing things for and by yourself that you never dreamed possible. You may also realize that you have begun to think differently about yourself and the world in which you live.

At this point in the process, you may begin thinking, "I just may live through this loss . . . no, I WILL live through this loss!" You now have proof that you do have the ability and resources to move ahead and live life, albeit a different life than before. You may also think, "I will incorporate this loss into the fabric of my life and rebuild a new one."

These changes in thought are essential to asserting yourself as a person capable of good mourning. Once you begin to change your thought processes, your feelings about your future and your possibilities will follow.

You may experience any number of emotions as you encounter the prospects of moving on; at first, you may feel anxiety, fear, sadness, or longing, but later you may experience excitement, anticipation, feelings of success, and accomplishment as you become increasingly more comfortable with the new you. Once your thoughts and feelings confirm your ability to move on, they will be expressed in positive actions.

A word of caution here is that there are a few hurdles that must be overcome in this choice. These hurdles are temptation, fear, and selection.

Temptation

The first hurdle you must face is the temptation to remain a victim of your loss. Feelings of victimization are common to those who have faced the death of a loved one; nothing brings feelings of victimization to the surface more. You may ask such questions as, *Why us? Why Now? What did I do to deserve this?* You feel out of control, picked on, or used in a cruel sort of way.

Generally, there are individuals around who can and will lend support as you work to make sense of this senseless intrusion into your life. Often, these folks will be around for long periods of time and find real personal comfort in taking care of you in your distress. Admittedly, it feels good to have people around who can and will take care of you and your family. As good as this feels, however, it is not in your best interest to be completely taken care of for the rest of your life. Remaining the victim of the loss means that you must constantly keep your supply of caretakers full. It means that you must always find people who are willing to feel sorry for you, pity your plight, and step in and do things for you. It means that you will spend most of your energy building a wall of human beings who will help you keep the reality from getting through and keep you from taking responsibility for your own life. So although there is a certain amount of comfort in the victim role for a time, the truth is that this role can be debilitating.

When you cross the hurdle of remaining the victim or helpless mourner, you run the risk of having to face the situation completely and become responsible for yourself. This can be both frightening and disconcerting, which is why the temptation to remain the victim of your loss is so great.

You may not always know what to do or how to respond in every situation. Indeed, you may make some mistakes. On the surface, it might appear easier to have someone else take responsibility for your life. You would always have someone else to blame if or when things did not go exactly right. Yet, once you cross this hurdle of temptation and decide to not remain the victim, you will be ready to risk taking responsibility for yourself, a risk essential to your survival and progress.

Fear

The fear of how others might respond to you asserting yourself as a new, different, and responsible person is the second hurdle that must be crossed. You may find yourself worrying about how friends, family members, social acquaintances, work associates, or society in general will respond to the you that is emerging as a result of your mourning process. Your perceptions of how others see your progress can be very powerful in keeping you from moving on.

Realize that people will have advice about everything you are facing and deciding. Most people who give advice expect you to follow it without question and may become angry if you do not. It is easy for others to criticize your decisions and actions from the outside—they are not living your experience. You may find that this pressure of worrying about how others might respond to your changes will keep you from doing things you want to do. Not only are you faced with your fear about how they will respond, you are also fearful of not doing the right thing.

It is important for you to realize that the death of your loved one has not just affected your life, it has affected others around you as well. Often people will seek to exert pressure on you to keep you where you are for their own purposes. They may feel uncomfortable with the changes they perceive taking place in you. They may even feel pressure to change their own responses to life because of your changes. However, you must not allow the fear of how others might respond to your changes to deter you from moving on with your life. Your life is *yours* to live! You have the sole responsibility for how it will be lived. Only you can truly decide how to handle your life. Crossing this hurdle is difficult, but once it is done, it can open doors to continued healthy mourning as well as healthier perspectives on your abilities to care for yourself and your situation.

Selection

The third hurdle is closely connected to the previous two. It involves the selection of support systems consistent with your assertion to move ahead with your life. Often, an examination of your life will reveal patterns of interacting in relationships that are unhealthy or less productive than you desire. As you discover how you want to live life, you must also work to build support for the positive changes you are making.

Again, people who made up your support system prior to the death of your loved one may or may not agree with your new approach to life. They may not always act honestly or objectively in what they tell you or recommend for you. They may have their own personal agendas as they relate to you. Individuals who have lost a spouse, for example, find that some friends will always see them as part of a couple and will never be able to accept the change brought about by the loss. They can also be resistant to other changes, such as the addition of a new relationship or spouse at some later point in time.

Remember, you are the producer and director of your new life. You are the lead actor. It is up to you to decide who will play the supporting roles in your new life. Provided your new directions are not harmful to you or others, it is imperative that your supporting cast agrees with your new directions. This means that you may have to focus less attention on those who would rather keep you in your place, shifting your focus instead toward those who are capable of helping you move along your new, chosen paths.

You will have to learn to ask for what you want and need. Growth should be your new directive, and support consistent with that growth will be necessary in your work of mourning. Therefore, you must begin to free yourself of hindrances—thoughts, perceptions, and people—that would keep you from achieving your goals and begin to rely on support systems consistent with positive change and growth.

The Choice to Begin Rebuilding

The third choice in the Mid-Mourning Phase is to Begin Rebuilding. An allusion has already been made to the similarities between facing the death of a loved one and facing the devastation of a natural disaster. The allusion may be carried a step further to include deciding what directions to pursue in the aftermath of such a disaster. After sorting through debris and the massive cleanup involved, comes rebuilding.

Individuals who have dealt with the aftermath of a natural disaster know the importance of putting life back together in practical ways. They must consider when to rebuild, how to go about it, where to relocate in the interim, what resources are available, how those resources will be used, and what avenues are open to them via insurance settlements and/or loans. This is an enormous task. Eventually, most people find ways to begin the rebuilding process. They find the strength and vision necessary to dream, plan, and start over.

The same is true for you as you face the third choice of the Mid-Mourning Phase of grief. You have experienced the devastation of the loss event and have worked at evaluating and sorting through your relationship and life. You have begun addressing the painful realities of life without your loved one. You possess those experiences, memories, and shared values that provide comfort and direction as you move on. You are ready to begin rebuilding your new life. You are facing the what, when, where and how questions that accompany any rebuilding project. The only difference is that you are answering these questions with your life on the line. As you gather from all the resources you have access to, the need for blueprints and models of what you want to build becomes clear.

No rebuilding project worth the effort can be done without some sort of planning and testing. And it is no different with your life. The choice to Begin Rebuilding starts with developing blueprints and constructing models of how you envision the end product. The questions of what kind of life you want, what you want to do, where you want to be, and how you intend to get there are all part of this process. This choice involves dreaming, projecting into the future, and visualizing the blueprints and models.

My grandfather was a carpenter—an artisan, builder, and inventor. He took pride in his work, whether it was the repair of a cabinet door or the construction of a home from the ground up. As a boy, I was amazed at how skilled he was at his craft. Sometimes I would catch him sitting in his rocking chair at the end of a day's work, staring off into space. "Grandpop," I would ask, "what are you doing?" His attention would shift to my question, and he would say something like, "Oh, I'm just thinking about the house I'm building."

I never fully appreciated that process until I was older. Although I never was able to step inside his mind, I know that he was dreaming, projecting, and visualizing how to build the house to his specifications. He constantly worked from blueprints and models. He would never hesitate to change or alter a blueprint or plan if what he tried did not produce the intended outcome. He was innovative and a risk taker. He believed in his abilities, his dreams, and his products. If he was afraid of failure, he hardly ever let it show. When something did not work out the way he envisioned, he would go back to the drawing board and start again. He made mistakes and miscalculations at times—he was not perfect. Yet, in each project, he worked at making it match his vision.

The choice to Begin Rebuilding requires that you draw up blueprints and construct models as well. It is a time of dreaming and visualizing about what you want your life to be from this point forward. It is a choice to try on new roles and ideas that have emerged as you have reflected on your life. It is a time to begin extending beyond yourself into the world around you, a world that is very different than it was before. It is a time to risk asserting the new you and your new plans. You can accomplish this rebuilding process through conversations with friends and family members; attending and sharing in support groups; and, when necessary, working with other people who can help you realize your plans.

This is also a time when you may experience some ambivalence because you are not quite finished dealing with the past. Guilt for moving on, feelings of betrayed loyalties, and the influences of self-perception prior to the loss can surface at times, causing you to question your new directions. Yet, what is most important is that you work to regain a sense of balance, integrating the loss into your life in a way that allows you to move forward.

Many times, you may find yourself going back to the drawing board, reworking your blueprints, and altering your models. You too will make mistakes and miscalculations from time to time. That is okay. The point is that you are engaging in active involvement with the world and testing your discoveries and dreams. It can be frightening and invigorating at the same time. I encourage you to dream and work. As you do this, you will discover that you are rebuilding your life and you can feel satisfaction from your successes. You are participating in Good Mourning.

The choices of Mid-Mourning flow naturally from the associated challenges of this transition phase. The single word "change" best defines the choices of this phase. Purposeful, planned change will guide you through the challenges inherent during this time of transition. The three choices of the Mid-Mourning Phase that will help establish your new directions are:

- **The Choice to Be Alone** — necessary to gain wisdom for your journey.

- **The Choice to Assert Yourself** — necessary for self-empowerment.

- **The Choice to Begin Rebuilding** — necessary to establish life purpose.

Snapshots from My Personal Journey

"I can't do this anymore! I just can't do this!" Those words issued from a very deep place in my soul in the wee hours of the morning barely three months after Christy's death. I often had trouble sleeping in those first few months. I was desperately lonely, especially at night. The depth of my grief often gnawed more intensely at my insides during the darkest hours of the day.

In an effort to medicate my loneliness and pain, I became involved in a relationship that was not the healthiest in the world. As with any substance intended to dull pain, when the effects wore off, I convinced myself that I needed more. In my heart, I knew I was headed down a pointless path, but I had difficulty turning back. In the early hours of that pivotal morning, I came face-to-face with the realization that the path of least resistance was more often than not the path to destruction. I would have none of that! I realized that being alone was different from being lonely and that I needed to make decisions based on discoveries revealed in my alone times and not my lonely ones. That day I severed the relationship and got back on the path of healing.

~~~

"Are you sure you want to do that? That just seems like it will take too much time and effort!" I often heard those statements in response to assertions I made related to my intents and purposes. In fact, the first one came on the day of the memorial service at Christy's school. In Christy's memory and honor, I wanted to set up an endowed scholarship for future educators at the University of North Texas. I was amazed that what I felt was a logical step was met with resistance. That experience made me aware of two very important realities: first, I must tap the courage to make statements of purpose, and second, not everyone will accept those assertions with open arms. That day marked the first but certainly not the last time I heard, "Are you sure you want to do that? That just seems like it will take too much time and effort!"

~~~

I slept little the night before. My stomach churned when I finally did crawl out of bed. My nerves were raw. I was scared to death, scared that I would not be able to do it, scared that others would laugh at me, scared that I had made a big mistake. I was just plain scared. What was the source of my fear? I was headed back to college—thirty-six years old and headed back to college! Now it might not have been so bad if I were starting in graduate level courses; there would likely be folks my age in grad school, but I had to spend a year taking classes for undergrads. Some of those classes were freshman-level courses. I knew that in order to add teaching credentials to my degree, I had to make up certain deficiencies in education classes, but I would be on campus and in class with eighteen- to twenty-year-olds—I was petrified!

I remember almost staying home, yet I knew that I had to face my fears, walk through them, and do what was necessary; otherwise, fear would win. My decision to step foot on campus that June morning was merely the first of many explorations into what I wanted to do as I rebuilt my life. It was part of my plan. Later that month, I took the GRE and was accepted to grad school to pursue my counseling degree. I often wonder where I would be now if I had succumbed to my fears that morning. I'm certainly glad I didn't.

~~~

Questions for Reflection

- List three personal insights that you have discovered, rediscovered, or affirmed thus far in your process of mourning.

- In what ways have these discoveries empowered you to move purposefully forward in your mourning?

- In what areas do you foresee the most challenge to your rebuilding process? How do you anticipate addressing these specific challenges?

Late Mourning—The Continuation

The Panhandle region of Texas is famous (or infamous, as the case may be) for the tornadoes that sweep through the countryside each spring. Having grown up in that part of the country, I was used to being rudely awakened in the middle of the night by high winds, torrential rain, hail, loud crashing thunder, and blinding lightning that momentarily froze the pitch black landscape into eerie snapshots of powerless houses, windblown trees, and flying debris. The storm siren would sound, and my family would dash for the storm cellar, hoping that the threatening tornado would not carry us away before we reached safety. I remember my family, on countless occasions, huddling together in the cellar built by my grandfather, wondering what was happening to everything above ground.

After the storm had passed, we would return to the house and go back to bed. Although I went to bed, I rarely slept the rest of the night. I would lie awake anticipating the dawn, anxious to see how the storm had changed the town and surrounding areas. *Had anything been blown away? Had there been a flood at the creek in the park? Had anyone been injured or killed? Was there major damage? Would there be changes?*

I would think that morning would never arrive, but it always did, and as the dawn crept into my room, I knew that I could begin to explore the aftermath of the storm. I was always relieved to see the sun begin brightening the sky. I knew that no matter what had happened the night before, I was alive and the storm had passed. I had another day to live, explore, and grow.

The beginning of the Late Mourning Phase of grief is similar to waiting for the dawn following a night of stormy weather. You have been rudely awakened by the storm of the loss event, and you feel terrified because of the devastation around you. You realize that one whom you love did not make it through the storm, and you are left trembling at the prospect of facing the world without your loved one.

You think that the dawn will never break, that you will remain in darkness and uncertainty forever. You ponder how you will go on with life. You wonder if you will ever be able to live a normal life again. You spend time thinking about how life was before the event and how it will be different now. You even begin planning how you will approach getting on with your life. Yet you are still waiting for the dawn, so you can begin exploring your world in earnest.

Eventually, whether suddenly or gradually, you will realize that dawn has indeed come, and although things are different—you are different—you have the chance to begin living the life you have constructed during the transition. Life does in fact go on, and you are a part of that life. You have responsibilities to yourself and the world around you. You have opportunities to create something unique through your efforts.

The night is over and the day has come. Now you can begin to explore, grow, and experience life as a person who has survived and is determined to live successfully following loss.

The Characteristics of Late Mourning

The Late Mourning Phase of the grief process focuses on the continuation of life following loss. It is important to remember that the various feelings associated with grief may be experienced at any point in the process of mourning. For example, you may discover that you experience anger or sadness during any phase, however, that anger or sadness may be for different reasons connected with your loss and may vary in intensity in each phase.

As you enter Late Mourning, you will discover that the three characteristics most closely associated with this phase focus less on feelings of grief and more on attitudes and perceptions as they relate to moving on with your life.

An Attitude of Acceptance

Acceptance of your loss and life situation is vital in your ability to move on with life in healthy ways; however, the prevailing attitude of acceptance necessary to accomplish this does not come all at once.

Some who work in the field of grief inadvertently communicate that acceptance is a state of mind to be achieved, a goal toward which individuals strive. In my thinking and experience, this tends to communicate that acceptance of your loss, your situation, your changed life and its accompanying possibilities, awaits you at the end of some magical rainbow. It appears to say that once you reach this special place in time, you will experience acceptance.

I disagree with this notion. I do not believe that acceptance is a goal to be attained. On the contrary, acceptance is the motivating force that helps get you *through* the process of mourning. It is the daily process of working to accept the reality of your situation through healthy expressions of your grief. It is the affirmation of your personhood, your life, and your possibilities through demonstrations of lessons learned and insights gained in the process.

Acceptance is a gradual process that must be worked at each day. You will not suddenly arrive at the destination of acceptance and be okay. You will work at it each day and ultimately develop a prevailing attitude of acceptance that may be more readily transferred as you deal with loss issues in other areas of your life as well.

Many physicians and nurses recognize the importance of daily work with acceptance and affirmation in the healing of abdominal surgery patients. Individuals who have experienced abdominal surgery are encouraged to begin walking soon after the surgery in order to facilitate timely healing. Although it is difficult in the beginning, patients discover that by walking, they heal more quickly and completely and are able to affirm their abilities to take care of themselves.

The same principal applies to the process of acceptance. As you work each day to affirm your life, you will heal more completely and empower yourself to access your resiliencies as you create a new life.

Integration of the Loss into Your Life-Scheme

A second characteristic is that of integration of the loss into your life-scheme. As you work at the daily process of acceptance and affirmation, you will be integrating the loss into your life as well. Integration is essential for healthy reconciliation in that it allows you to be in touch with your own pain associated with loss as well as the pain of others who find themselves in similar circumstances. One who has fully integrated loss through the process of acceptance and affirmation may be better equipped to mourn future personal losses and assist others as they mourn losses as well.

A prevailing attitude of acceptance and the integration of your loss, however, do not mean that you are immune to surges or spikes of grief from time to time. An individual who has fully integrated loss is still likely to be swept up by feelings of grief on occasion. This experience is common and to be expected. Once you have been sensitized to the pain of loss, it is difficult to escape its effects. You may find yourself inundated with feelings of sadness or longing or fear in certain situations. Various triggers can cause these feelings to surface. Do not be afraid of them. Holidays, places or activities that were special to you and your loved one, aromas, sounds, another person's loss, songs, and so forth can all serve as triggers for these momentary surges of grief. It is perfectly normal to experience them. In fact, these surges may help you monitor your progress as they happen from time to time throughout the rest of your life.

The key to remember is that feelings of grief will no longer dominate you at this point in the process. You will have come to a place where you are comfortable with your feelings of grief as well as the grief experiences of others. This freedom from domination by grief can serve to empower you as you embrace the third characteristic of the Late Mourning Phase.

Emergence of a Present-Tense Focus

The third characteristic associated with the Late Mourning Phase of the grief process is that of the emergence of a present-tense focus. Up to this point, you have spent much of your time and energy reflecting on the past and wondering about the future. You may have looked back on your life with your loved one with mixed feelings of guilt, anger, regret, relief, joy, pride, or longing. You may have projected yourself into the future, experiencing fear, uncertainty, anticipation, anxiety, or excitement. But as you move into this new phase, you will begin to realize that you are ready to face your life in the here and now.

You may recognize that the past cannot be changed or altered—only your perceptions can be—and that the future is yet to be determined. You may realize more than ever before that guarantees do not exist and that anticipated tomorrows might never arrive. You may even recognize just how precious life is and come to value your place in it in ways new to you. In this third phase, you experience an emerging focus on the present tense of life.

In the present-tense focus, you may find yourself experiencing a heightened sense of the immediate, not wanting to let things pass you by. You may be more aware of sights, sounds, beauty, people, relationships, and the parts they play in your life. You will likely focus on issues that are more immediate in nature. As you continue to accept, affirm, and integrate the loss into your life, you will be able to spend more of your emotional, mental, physical, and spiritual energy on today. You will realize that today is the only day you are guaranteed and that you will work to fill your present moments with meaningful activity.

I do not mean that you must attempt to do everything all at once, but you will find yourself working within the framework of today to accomplish the goals you have set. You will see the need for balance and priorities in your life, and you will seek out the people and activities that assist you in creating them.

Your accomplishments will find fruition in all of your todays, never in the yesterdays or tomorrows of life. You will discover how to learn and draw from the past as well as how to plan your future as you live in the here and now!

The Late Mourning Phase of the grief process focuses on the continuation of life following loss. The three characteristics most closely associated with this phase focus less on feelings of grief and more on attitudes and perceptions as they relate to moving on with your life. You will recognize shifts in thinking and acting consistent with the following characteristics:

- **An Attitude of Acceptance**

- **Integration of the Loss into Your Life-Scheme**

- **Emergence of a Present-Tense Focus**

"A picture is worth a thousand words!" We've all heard that expression, and in many respects, it is true. Words are sometimes easy to forget, but pictures tend to stay with us in ways words don't. As I moved through the transition time, conducting my own personal work of mourning, I was compelled to find ways to communicate my discoveries that would make sense to others, was of connecting the process of grief and mourning to real life. Several pictures, diagrams, conceptualizations, and models emerged because of this process. One model that sums up the process of the characteristics of Late Mourning follows:

LIFE

Loss

LOSS

Life

In essence, this picture communicates that life is bigger than loss, a fact that often escapes conscious contemplation. We tend to live life as if loss were an alien experience—one that happens to others, but not to us. That false assumption works fine until it doesn't anymore, until we find ourselves the victim of loss, and then loss *is* bigger than life. Loss dominates our world. It is all we see, feel, taste, touch, or experience. It threatens to dwarf anything and everything life has to offer.

Now society has a tendency to push us toward one of two stances. Society is comfortable with us going back and pretending that life is bigger than loss again. That stance is one of the main sources of those magical timelines to which we often find ourselves enslaved—the magical six months, year, or two years. The other stance society is comfortable with is when we can define our lives only by the loss we have experienced. They want to box us into the loss is bigger than life position, thereby freezing us into a prescribed set of beliefs, behaviors, and roles.

Ultimately, the healthy outcome of Good Mourning is twofold. First, we become reconciled to the loss we have experienced as we work through the process of bringing together what we thought we had in life to what we really have. Second, we experience integration of that loss and its lessons into the fabric of our lives, thereby making the lessons learned readily accessible as we encounter other losses. The most lasting and meaningful connections we make with others are always at the point of their pain and never at the point of their victory. Reconciliation and integration of life losses empowers us to truly make a difference.

Questions for Reflection

- If someone came to you asking your advice about learning to accept the death of a loved one, what would you say? In what direction would you suggest they work?

- How would you describe "integration" as it relates to mourning a death loss? Draw a representation of what integration means to you in this context and share that drawing with another person.

- Living in the here and now empowers us to focus on the importance of the present. C.S. Lewis wrote in *The Screwtape Letters*, "The Present is the point at which time touches eternity!" Write three examples of how the present is more meaningful to you now and share those thoughts with a friend.

The Challenges of Late Mourning

In the Late Mourning Phase, facing the world with enhanced perspectives, new directions, and strengthened resolve will command your attention. It will be as though you are a butterfly emerging from your chrysalis.

In Early Mourning Phase, you are very vulnerable and need to discover how to take care of yourself very much like a caterpillar does. You feel in need of protection and support from forces greater and stronger than you are. You need to find healthy ways to begin the mourning process.

Fairly soon after your loss and your early mourning, you move into the Mid-Mourning Phase, which may be likened to the caterpillar's construction of the chrysalis. In much the same manner that the butterfly-to-be goes through a metamorphosis unseen by human eyes, you begin the process of reflection, change, integration, and healing—much of which you accomplish in the private moments of personal mourning and grief work. This is the transition phase of the grief process. As those who have gone through the transition know, this process can be grueling and excruciatingly painful at times and cannot be rushed.

Once you create the structure of what you want to become, you will begin the process of emerging from the chrysalis—entering the continuation of your life in the Late Mourning Phase of your grief. However painless and effortless you might like this emergence to be, there will still be effort and struggle. Although the butterfly possesses all the potential of a creature ready to fly, this new creation must struggle and push and work to free itself from the chrysalis before flight is possible. This process is necessary, for if the butterfly remains encased in its chrysalis, it will die. Likewise, if the butterfly receives too much assistance while emerging, it will not have the strength to live as intended; it must emerge from its chrysalis on its own or perish.

This emergence to continuation has three challenges that must be faced. During this phase, you will be challenged to Redefine Closure, Work on a Life Plan, and Prepare for Setbacks.

Redefine Closure

Closure has been defined as a closing or shutting up, a conclusion. These definitions tend to carry with them the picture of something tied up neatly—a package with definite boundaries and parameters. Human beings tend to view closure of relationships and events this way. But these definitions may sometimes cause you to believe that all experiences you face may be tied up in packages, never to be unwrapped again. This type of belief system may set you up for disappointment and disillusionment along the way, especially in the grief process.

Relationships and events such as the death of a loved one are not easily tied up in packages, and the conclusions are not always as clear-cut as you might desire them to be. With that in mind, we must redefine closure in order to better facilitate your continuation with life following loss.

Instead of visualizing closure as tying things up in packages, it may be more beneficial to view the process as taking place in a chemistry lab where you place your experiences in glass test tubes. There are two advantages to viewing closure in this way.

First is the realization that experiences, such as the death of a loved one, have long-term effects on your life, and you will be faced with questions about them at various times throughout your life. These questions and feelings associated with a particular experience will bubble up in your conscious thoughts randomly or as a result of triggers. This can be rather disconcerting if you view feelings and experiences as things never to be dealt with again once they have been wrapped up. But when you view closure as an ongoing study, a test tube process, you open the door for experimenting with your feelings in a way that brings understanding and the ability to visualize the experiences and memories that react within you.

In a laboratory, when you face an unknown, you pull out chemicals, test tubes, beakers, and Bunsen burners, and work away at them until you collect enough evidence to back up your hypothesis. In mourning, when you come up against emotional perplexities or when you feel internal conflict, pulling them off the shelf, and devoting your attention to them will help you understand them better and work with them better.

An unlabeled bottle of mixed chemicals, when placed up on a shelf, remains an unknown. But when you take it down and perform extractions and separations and tests, you can determine exactly what the chemical makeup is. Similarly, if we simply bottle up our emotions and place them up on the shelf, as you would under the traditional concept of closure, you stand the risk of emotional combustion. At any time, emotions can bubble up, and if we are not ready to get to the root of the source or access our deep hurts, we stand little chance of ever having control of our emotions.

In the test tube process, typically all that is necessary is simply acknowledging the feelings associated with your experiences and reaffirming any original decisions. If you view closure as a test tube process, you will not be surprised when thoughts, feelings, or experiences bubble up in your mind. You will expect that they will pop up from time to time and be somewhat prepared for them. You will be able to ask exploratory questions, such as, *"Has anything changed since I last thought about this situation?"* or *"Do I need to investigate the situation further at this point?"* This attitude allows you to tell yourself what it is you want or need to do with a situation at the time it comes up. If you do not need to do anything with the thought, feeling, or situation, you may simply acknowledge it and move on. If, on the other hand, you need to reevaluate the situation or feeling and add any new insight, you have the opportunity to do so.

The second advantage to viewing closure as a test tube lies in the fact that there will be times when new information or insights will become available to you through the processes of growth and investigation. In this way, your healing will not reach a static point but will continue evolving and improving in different ways throughout your life.

If you practice treating your closure as a test tube process, you will learn to recall at will, an event or experience as well as any feeling connected with it. You will then be able to determine whether the new information alters your perceptions or any decisions connected to the experience, and you will be able to take appropriate action to incorporate the new information into your life framework. If the new information or insight does not affect the original closure of the experience, you have not lost anything at all by reviewing it.

In short, to redefine closure in the manner described is to define it as an ongoing process, a view that may facilitate continued personal growth rather than a rigid box with well-defined limits that are resistant to exploration. The redefinition may help you face the winds of life like a willow tree that has the ability to bend and move with the flow, rather than being like a rigid oak tree that resists the wind. In grieving, only the flexible survive and continue to grow.

Work on a Life Plan

The importance of developing a Life Plan during this phase of your mourning cannot be underestimated. The concept of continuation carries with it the ideas of stability and survival. You are a survivor; you will create a certain sense of stability in your life as you move through the process of mourning.

The challenge of developing a Life Plan proceeds naturally from this sense of being a survivor as well as the stability you work to create. You will have already participated in the process of forming a tentative direction for your life during the Mid-Mourning Phase of this process by deciding to assert yourself and begin rebuilding. You will have created and tested various blueprints and models, seeking a comfortable direction in which to move. Finally, you are called upon to develop those dreams and models into a more formalized Life Plan, which will serve as the new overall goal for your life.

I remember the first time I was confronted with the contemplation of my Life Plan following Christy's death. I was visiting with my friend and life insurance agent in his office when he said, "I would ask you what you are going to do now, but that is not the question I want to ask you. Instead, I want to ask, 'What do you **want** to do now?'"

No one had asked me that question. Typically, the questions people asked were tinted with pessimism and uncertainty. This question carried an empowering component. I was quiet for a moment, and before I really knew what was happening, I responded, "I want to write, speak, and teach!" That seminal response formed the framework around which I began to restructure both my mourning and my eventual Life Plan.

I knew that for my life to be of use and worth to myself, my daughter, and anyone else who entered it, I would have to involve myself in healthy grief work. I knew that if I wanted my writing, speaking, and teaching to contribute to the well-being of others, it would be necessary for me to learn how to mourn my loss in healthy and effective ways. Obviously, my Life Plan grew and became more all-encompassing to include new relationships, remarriage, and expanding my professional pursuits to become a psychotherapist, but the important point here is that I began to work on a Life Plan.

The development of a Life Plan involves the following distinct aspects: your overall dream or goal; your statement of purpose or intent; your strategy or action steps; and your measure of progress.

Step One Asks: *What Do You Want to Do?*

The first step in developing and pursuing your overall dream or goal involves the question my friend asked me—*What do you want to do?* As you work on this part of your Life Plan, it will be helpful for you to verbalize your thoughts to others who have an interest in you and the ability to remain objective about your statements. It may also be helpful for you to write down your dreams and goals to get a handle on what it is you really do want to do, become, create, have, or enjoy. You might begin by completing the following statement: "In the area of (   ), I want to . . ." This may help you formulate your thoughts into the beginnings of your Life Plan. Be as detailed as you wish in describing your dream or goal.

Step Two Asks: *What Are the Parts of Your Dream or Goal?*

The second step involves breaking down your dream into its various parts. In my experience, I discovered that in order to teach, I had to go back to college and obtain a teaching certificate. This became one of my statements of purpose or intent. It went something like this: "In order to teach, I must enroll in college and meet the requirements for teaching certification." I went through this process with each part of my overall dream or goal. For me, this part of the process was exciting and challenging. As you begin work on your Life Plan, you may find this experience to be an exciting challenge as well.

In some cases, however, rather than breaking down a goal, you may decide to redefine the plan altogether. This too is an important part of the process. As you move ahead, you will continue to clarify, reevaluate, and update you dreams as well as how you plan to achieve them.

Step Three Asks: *What Strategies Will You Employ, or What Action Steps Will You Take?*

The third step requires you to specify the strategies or action steps that will help you accomplish each statement of purpose or intent. This becomes the "how" for each statement.

Before I would be able to complete my defined goal, I would have to investigate the entrance requirements to the university, discover any deficiencies I had to make up in my coursework, and understand the requirements for state certification beyond the coursework and time invested. This information became a part of my strategy to teach. In all, I discovered that my certification could be accomplished in one year.

In your own life, consider the steps you will need to take to make your statements of purpose a reality. *How much time or money will it require? What other resources or support do I need in order to accomplish my purpose? What known obstacles exist that I can address at the beginning of my project?*

A statement of purpose will serve you better if **you write it down**. It will help you focus your efforts and serve as a tool for those you choose as mentors or accountability partners in your endeavors.

Step Four Asks: *How Will You Measure Your Progress?*

The fourth and final step in the development of your Life Plan focuses on measuring your progress. In this step, you will ask yourself various qualifying questions, such as: *How will I know whether I have finished this particular part of my plan? What do I need to do differently to reach my goal if one strategy should fail? How does my strategy need to be altered?* This step will help you to check your progress, reminding you that you are in control of your responses and choices as you move forward.

Rarely will a particular statement of purpose be attained without some degree of reevaluation and change. When you meet resistance to your goals, the temptation will be to ask why you are facing a challenge. A common problem with the why questions is that there is a tendency to place blame on someone or something else for the problem or challenge encountered. Asking why drains precious energy from your pursuit and clouds your focus.

Instead, it is better to ask, "What can I do differently or change in order to attain my goal?" This approach causes you to think in terms of options and possibilities rather than in rigid, liner terms when it comes to meeting your goals. The important point to remember is that you are constantly checking your progress. This gives you control of how you work on your plan.

I employed this four-step process for each area of my Life Plan as it related to speaking, writing, teaching, public school counseling, and licensure as a professional psychotherapist. I continue to use this formula as I work toward new parts of my Life Plan today.

I have included a set of worksheets as a part of Appendix D that will allow you to work on creating a Life Plan.

Prepare for Setbacks

Surprises can either be fun and exciting or frustrating and disappointing. Depending on your past experience with surprises, you may either welcome or shy away from them. Surprises in the form of setbacks can be very disappointing and disheartening. It would be wonderful if the world would welcome your efforts to rebuild your life with open arms; however, that is not always the case. For this reason, it is imperative that you face the challenge of Preparing for Setbacks, for they will inevitably come.

Sometimes these setbacks will come from friends and family members who make statements—whether intentional or unintentional—that discourage your efforts to rebuild. Other times, the setbacks will come from within as you struggle with thoughts, attitudes, and feelings that have been debilitating in other similar situations in your past. Still other setbacks have their origins in bureaucratic rules and regulations or natural circumstances. These setbacks can affect you emotionally, mentally, spiritually, and physically, depending on their source.

The key to handling setbacks lies in being prepared for their occurrence. I am not saying that you must be able to anticipate each setback. Rather, you will do yourself a favor if you simply accept the fact that they *will* happen. The acceptance of this reality may keep you from feeling so devastated when they do come. Because you are successfully working through your loss, you will be better prepared to face the setbacks ahead as you continue to live. Preparation softens the surprise element of setbacks.

In the Late Mourning Phase, facing the world with enhanced perspectives, new directions, and strengthened resolve will command your attention. It will be as though you are a butterfly emerging from your chrysalis. The challenges associated with the Late Mourning Phase shift the focus of your life from transition to continuation. These three challenges require you to:

- **Redefine Closure**

- **Work on a Life Plan**

- **Prepare for Setbacks**

These challenges involve mental, emotional, and practical components as you prepare to continue with life in definitive ways. Establishing firm understandings in all three areas can help create the framework for a successful continuation of your life.

Who would have ever thought that a personal epiphany could occur in the middle of a life insurance agent's office? I certainly did not! Yet, that is exactly what happened when Ted Cantrell asked me, "What do you *want* to do, Mark?" Ted and I had been friends for a few years, but the experience of Christy's death brought us closer, forged a friendship that is more valuable and viable than if we were blood relations.

That seminal question opened my mind and heart to the exploration of life in ways I never dreamt possible. Since that time, Ted and I have met regularly to not only shoot the breeze, but to serve as sounding boards for each other as well. In every meeting we have, that question finds its way into our conversation in both subtle and obvious ways. That question was perhaps the second most important turning point in my life related to Christy's death.

~~~

Questions for Reflection

- Prior to reading this section of the book, what was your definition or understanding of the meaning of "closure"? How has the definition of closure mentioned here altered your perception of this process?

- As you prepare to work on your Life Plan, what area or areas do you anticipate addressing in the process?

- What do you want to do? Express your answer in a single sentence that summarizes your intent.

- On what personal strength do you depend most when facing setbacks?

The Choices of Late Mourning

The choices associated with the Late Mourning Phase may be classified as choices of extension and expansion. These are appropriate qualifiers in that they convey a sense of growth, adventure, change, and risk. Nothing describes the choices of this phase better.

In this phase, you are in the midst of moving on with your life. You have worked diligently at learning to mourn in healthy ways. You are better equipped for this task. Yet even though you are better prepared, you may still feel a little anxious about your future because you do not know what awaits you as you venture forward.

I am reminded of **April 22, 1889** — the day designated as the Oklahoma Land Rush — where fifty to sixty thousand people congregated around the borders of that open expanse of land, awaiting the signal to begin their collective dash for free land in the Oklahoma Territory on which to stake their claim and begin building or rebuilding their dreams. Each individual, each family had pinned hopes on being able to find, claim, and hold on to prime real estate — the stuff of which dreams are made. When the shot rang out over the plains, setting the hopefuls on their way, the tension, anxiety, and excitement exploded in a rush of horses' hooves, shouts, and frantic activity! Dust billowed, hats flew, white-knuckled women hung on to their wagons, and children clung to each other for dear life as they bounced along in the back of buckboards and covered wagons. They were all seeking the same goal — a new life filled with promise and contentment.

You too are poised at a similar boundary. As you grasp the characteristics of this phase and understand the challenges that await you, you may realize that the choices that lie ahead are not for the faint of heart. These choices require work, perseverance, and endurance on your part. The territory before you is wild, unexplored, and full of possibility. It is up to you to discover, claim, and hold on to the things that will provide a full and meaningful life. It will be difficult at times, but the rewards can be so wonderful!

As you move into this territory, the choices you will face can provide you with the tools necessary to create the life of your design. In the Late Mourning Phase, you will be asked to choose to Engage Opposition, Keep Going, and Share Yourself with Others.

The Choice to Engage Opposition

This first choice relates specifically to the challenge of being prepared for setbacks in your attempts to rebuild your life. The fact of the matter is that you will encounter resistance and setbacks as you move forward — that is a given! You have already learned that being prepared for these experiences can help you mobilize your resources when faced with opposition. At this point, you must choose to engage the opposition in order to come out on top in this struggle.

The choice here may be likened to the scenario played out in the life of a professional athlete. Each week, the athlete prepares for the upcoming contest. The athlete knows that he or she will face opposition that is equally prepared and determined. The athlete must have a game plan designed to bring victory as well as alternative plans if the original does not work out as intended.

On the day of the contest, the athlete must step into the fray. The thrill, anticipation, anxiety, and uncertainty will cause the adrenaline to flow, and only action will alleviate the built-up tension. With all this in mind, can you imagine the athlete—as well-prepared as possible, goals and plans in place, dressed for the contest—deciding to stand on the sideline and not enter the game? That is almost unthinkable, isn't it? At the end of the game, everyone—including the athlete—would be left to wonder how the result would have been different if he or she had actually participated. Fear, uncertainty, or even lack of confidence can cause an athlete to refrain from participating, but the fact of the matter is that he or she has the choice to either face the competition or not.

At this point in the process of mourning, you are faced with a similar scenario. You are as prepared as possible, you have goals and plans in place, and you are ready to enter the game to win. The choice you face is whether you engage the opposition or not.

Remember, opposition to your progress and success is a given—this is just how life operates. You will never know how your plans will work unless you engage the opposition as it comes at you. There will be a certain amount of fear, anxiety, and questioning of your abilities as you move forward. You will never be able to determine how your life will turn out if you stand on the sideline and observe. You do not have a choice as to what kinds of situations life deals you; however, you do have a choice as to how you *respond* to those situations.

A choice to Engage Opposition is a choice to involve yourself in life. Nothing can be as frightening or rewarding! Remember, you are not alone in this choice. You will have built a support team of people who believe in change, growth, and you! Although your team will stand ready to assist you, only you can fill the slot labeled with your name as you engage the opposition.

The Choice to Keep Going

Endurance, perseverance, and determination come to mind when thinking about the second choice of the Late Mourning Phase of the grief process. At this point, you must choose to Keep Going! You must continue making choices as you move ahead with your life. This is likely not the first loss you have experienced, and it will not be the last. It is likely that this loss has caused the hurt from past losses to come to the surface as well, some of which you may not have fully mourned. You may have found yourself experiencing grief from several losses at one time, all triggered by this most recent one. But as you choose to keep making choices, you will gain wisdom for living. You will learn to face whatever comes next in your life more effectively.

In order to Keep Going in the process of rebuilding your life, it will be essential that you learn to do the next thing and learn to go the distance:

Learning to Do the Next Thing

I recall two things happening to me on the morning of Christy's death. The doctor came into the waiting room, looked at me, and said, "Mr. Hundley, I am sorry to tell you this . . . there is no easy way to tell you . . . but your wife is dead." Those words shook me to the very core of my being. I collapsed on the floor and wept—the disbelief, anger, bitterness, frustration, confusion, and fear pouring out of my soul intermingled with the tears streaming down my face. I was devastated! Completely undone! What would I do?

I lay there on the floor wanting nothing more than to disappear into the concrete below. I felt so alone, so powerless.

Then without warning, a voice from inside said, "Mark, there are lots of people here, and they don't know what to say and they don't know what to do. There are lots of decisions to be made, and the only one who can make those decisions is you, so get up and start making them now!" Almost without thought, I pulled myself from the floor. As I responded to this internal prompting and rose to sit on the sofa in the waiting room and face the doctor, a sense of peace and calm filled me. I was able to tap the inner strength necessary to do what came next.

As I sat there, my thoughts immediately raced back to the major points of a sermon presented by my college pastor back in February of 1974 entitled "In the Meantime." He referred to life's difficulties and interruptions as "meantimes," and facing the death of a loved one truly is a "mean time" in life! He outlined three things to do when life's meantimes intrude on our existence. He said that we must Lean Heavily on God, Lean Heavily on Our Family and Friends and finally, we must Do the Next Thing.

To illustrate the third point he said, "If you happen to be washing the dishes and your meantime comes and you have to leave the dishes in mid-wash to take care of the situation—as soon as you can, go back and finish washing the dishes." He gave this counsel with the intent of keeping us connected to the reality of living through the difficulties we face. Doing the next thing grounds us and helps us focus our attentions on accomplishing the tasks necessary for continuation.

In order to live successfully through the meantimes of life, we must learn to deal with the mean times we encounter while carrying on our responsibilities to self, family, and others at the same time. Life does not give us the luxury of either dealing with the mean time or taking care of responsibilities while the other challenge waits patiently in the wings. We must find ways to accomplish both. Learning to do the next thing can empower us to live this way. This choice demands marathon-type resolve.

Learning to Go the Distance

I have run two 26.2-mile marathons in my life. I remember the first time I contemplated participating in such an event, I could not envision finishing a distance that long. It was difficult enough to run two miles without stopping, much less 26.2! Nevertheless, I started the process of training and spent many long hours running in all types of weather just to prepare for the event. After several months of training, the day for my first marathon came. I was excited and apprehensive at the same time. I determined that I would finish the distance no matter what.

The marathon began, and I was having the time of my life! Things had been going well for twenty miles when I suddenly developed cramps in my calves. The pain was so intense at times that I wanted to stop and not finish the race at all. I later discovered that I had suffered a stress fracture in my left tibia in addition to the muscle cramps. Fortunately, two young friends had volunteered to meet me at mile eighteen to ensure that I finished the race. I was certainly glad they were there! They stopped with me and we would massage my calves and then continue until the next bout of cramps. The final six miles were completed in this manner. I *did* make it through the final distance, and the experience was incredible. In that one race, I learned a tremendous lesson about getting on with life following loss.

It became clear to me that a marathon is a metaphor of life. Goals, dreams, plans, effort, pain, setbacks, temptations to quit, self-doubt, feelings of optimism, accomplishment, and satisfaction at completion—all of these experiences were mine in the time it took me to run the course. The same may be said for living life following loss. The choice to Keep Going is the choice to go the distance, calling upon all the resources available while running the race. Once you have come this far in the process, Keep Going!

The Choice to Share Yourself with Others

I have often wondered what would have happened if Jonas Salk had decided not to share the information he discovered about fighting polio, or how life would be different if Louis Pasteur had kept his discoveries to himself. Where would we be today if Albert Einstein had given up experimenting and exploring after facing many failures? I am not sure these questions can be answered completely, but I do believe that life would be quite different if they had not shared their discoveries.

You will be in very much the same situation in the Late Mourning Phase. You will have traveled far into your journey through the land of mourning and will have gathered great insights and wisdom along the way. The path will have been long, grueling, and sometimes tedious. You will have faced many obstacles and successfully maneuvered your way through many treacherous waters. You will have been through forests of despair, deserts of loneliness, valleys of fear, and over mountains of doubt. At times, you will have found meadows of rest and springs of rejuvenation. You will have contemplated your future beside soothing reflection ponds. You will have found refuge in quiet caves of thought and introspection. You will have looked out over the plains of possibility and dreamed of your future. You will have participated in Good Mourning! It will then be time to face the choice to Share Yourself with Others.

Few experiences in life can be as anxiety-producing or as rewarding as sharing your life and experiences with others. On the one hand, you really cannot determine how people will respond to your openness and honesty. You see, people like you, have a story to tell, a story that can cause some to be encouraged and inspired while, at the same time, it can cause others to feel resentful and bitter. On the other hand, you are living in a society that tries to deny the reality of death and mourning. One who has successfully negotiated the tasks of mourning is likely to challenge the status quo.

With these things in mind, choosing to share yourself with others is still one of the best ways to keep yourself on track to healthy living, and it allows you to provide a model of success and encouragement to others when they face death and loss. One of the ways you can achieve and maintain emotional and mental health is by extending your focus beyond yourself into the lives of others.

Once you have reached this phase of mourning, you will truly have something of substance to share with other hurting individuals. You will understand the process through which they are going. You can identify with the struggles they are facing. You can empathize with their life experiences. You can be a wealth of information and support.

I encourage you to go beyond yourself and share your life with those suffering the pain of loss. Not only will you feel more fulfilled, you will help make the world a safer place to experience and express feelings of grief. You will be a pioneer in the field of healing from the pain of grief as you Share Yourself with Others!

The choices associated with the Late Mourning Phase may be classified as choices of extension and expansion. As you grasp the characteristics of this phase and understand the challenges that await you, you realize that the choices ahead are not for the faint of heart. These choices require work, perseverance, and endurance on your part. The choices of this final phase of the process are:

- **The Choice to Engage Opposition** — Know that you possess the power to respond.

- **The Choice to Keep Going** — Realize that working to stay connected to the reality of your situation and committing to go the distance will ultimately get you through.

- **The Choice to Share Yourself with Others** — Acknowledge that you have something of value to share with the world.

"Do the Next Thing, Mark! Do the Next Thing!" This simple phrase became my personal mantra and remains so to this day. I found power and courage in this phrase. From the moment the doctor delivered the news that Christy was dead, to my heart-wrenching conversation with Kacie, the power of this phrase connected me to the necessary. As we met with the funeral director, greeted visitors at the viewing and endured the pain of the funeral, this phrase bolstered my resolve.

"Do the Next Thing, Mark! Do the Next Thing!" As Kacie and I struggled to find ways to live meaningfully in the aftermath of Christy's death, this phrase served as a **guiding light. When I faltered**, fearing that I would be unable to take the next step in the process, this phrase calmed my fears and soothed my frayed nerves. When I explored the depths of my grief in quiet times of reflection, this phrase taught me patience. When I tentatively voiced my intended directions, this phrase boosted my resolve.

"Do the Next Thing, Mark! Do the Next Thing!" This simple phrase nudged me to reach out to others in ways I never had before, seeking wisdom, insight, and input so that my living could be more meaningful. When my life direction began to take shape, this phrase encouraged continuation. When a new friendship developed into a loving relationship that ultimately led to marriage, this phrase expanded my capacity to give and receive love. When Vanessa and I established our "family on the blend," this phrase opened the doors to greater love, empathy, and understanding.

"Do the Next Thing, Mark! Do the Next Thing!" As my life vision crystallized, this phrase served as a catalyst to live outside the box of convention and venture into areas of work I had never dreamt possible. This phrase has taught me that living successfully in the mean times of life is not only possible, but absolutely doable! This phrase has given me the ability to pay attention and walk circumspectly though life with a heart full of hope.

"Do the Next Thing, Mark! Do the Next Thing!" This simple phrase compelled me to write this book and drives my desire to share the healing power of Good Mourning with all who are open to its message. This simple phrase opened the door for me to join a group of professionals in founding the Journey of Hope Grief Support Center, a non-profit organization that provides free group grief support to children and families touched by the tragedy of death loss. This phrase reminds me that I have a message to share with the world, a message of hope and healing!

"Do the Next Thing, Mark! Do the Next Thing!" This simple phrase has found a home in Kacie's heart as well. She tapped the courage, determination, and perseverance necessary to mourn her mother's death and has established a life path that allows her to invest in the lives of young people. Kacie followed in her mother's footsteps and teaches high school English. This phrase weaves its way through the fabric of who she is as a person and infiltrates the lives of her students. They too are learning the power of doing the Next Thing.

"Do the Next Thing, Mark! Do the Next Thing!" This simple phrase has carried me through other losses and disappointments since Christy's death. This simple phrase will empower me to meet future losses as well. This simple phrase is my personal mantra for powerful living in the face of opposition. This simple phrase simply works!

Questions for Reflection

- In what ways have you already experienced opposition to the changes you are making in your life? What responses have been the most effective in empowering you to deal with the opposition faced thus far?

- In what ways has your faith or value system helped you stay connected to the situation in which you find yourself? How have your connections with others strengthened your ability to move through this process? What is the Next Thing you have done consistently to help you stay focused on your tasks of mourning?

- In what ways have you already found yourself sharing with others? In what areas do you anticipate being able to share your experiences in the future?

Preparing for Your Good Mourning Journey

A Personal Word of Encouragement

A journey of a million miles is taken in segments, not all at once. The same is true for the process of mourning the death of your loved one. You find yourself involved in a journey you didn't choose, which you are not adequately prepared for. Fortunately, you have the opportunity to invite others along as companions on this trip. You do not have to navigate what lies ahead of you all by yourself. You are not alone as you explore life after loss.

Although the direction your future takes is up to you and you alone, you can still benefit from the assistance of individuals, groups, organizations, and other resources. My experience tells me that people tend to work in healthier ways to reconcile themselves to their loss and integrate it into the fabric of their lives more effectively when assistance from others and a variety of resources is readily available. Once you understand that the overall direction and primary work is your responsibility, you are more likely to access the most appropriate resources for your trip and pack accordingly.

I don't know about you, but often when I travel, I find myself either over packing or taking the wrong items for my trip. Invariably, when I arrive at a destination, I have to buy something I forgot and then figure out a way to make room for that addition in my already overstuffed suitcase! Other times, I find myself wondering what I had been thinking when I decided to take all the stuff I didn't use. My advice to you as you embark on this journey is to pack for today, leaving room in your suitcase **for acquisitions as you progress.**

The items you pack for this trip form the basis of a positive support network that is so necessary as you travel the paths of mourning. I would like to suggest that you categorize what you pack into three support systems. The first system focuses on clarifying how you derive meaning from life through your personal beliefs and values. The second system holds the keys to the steps you take to access support from those around you. Finally the third system identifies the ways in which you draw upon your own personal strengths and resiliencies.

Support from Beliefs and Values

As you search for purpose and meaning in life, your beliefs and values will likely take on new importance. You may find yourself questioning and reevaluating long-held beliefs and values. This process is common, and I encourage you to explore your beliefs and values as completely as possible. Whether your values include a belief in God or some other higher power, a pursuit of humanitarian activities, or a search for individual discovery and growth, I urge you to involve yourself in strengthening this support system.

You might begin by attending the next meeting of an organization to which you belong or would like to belong. You may want to make an appointment with your minister, priest, or rabbi to discuss opportunities for discovery, growth, and eventually, service. You might consider keeping a journal detailing the processes through which you go as you create new purpose in life through the pursuit of your beliefs and values. Reading books that help you explore your faith and values often strengthens your personal beliefs. Participation in seminars or workshops can also foster growth, especially those focusing on values clarification or personal development.

Whatever you do, I encourage you to make room for the pursuit of your personal faith and values. This pursuit can contribute to healthy expressions of grief and can assist you in your reconciliation and continuation processes.

Support from Those Around You

The support you can receive from friends, family members, and your community is immeasurable. Make sure you leave plenty of room in this compartment for new acquisitions. This is the area most often overlooked in the process of adjusting to life after loss, but it can have tremendous impact on your healing. In addition to the moral and social support available in this support system, you will discover the immense practicalities hidden there as well.

To benefit, you must learn to access these resources, as they exist in your particular community. Friends and family members are typically the first group to whom you turn in times of crisis. In addition to those tried and true resources, you might also want to consider support from clergy, attorneys, physicians, funeral directors, financial consultants, and professional counselors or therapists. Organizations such as churches, synagogues, temples, and service organizations often provide support resources beyond the obvious. Check out the resources offered by local colleges, universities, or continuing-education centers. Hospitals, health clubs, and spas offer very practical and supportive services as well. All of these and many more make up potential resources of support from those around you. I encourage you to begin expanding this support system to give yourself even more options as you progress.

Support from Within

In the midst of this difficult situation, you cannot afford to sit back and passively wait for something to happen to make you better or for someone to do for you the things only you have the capacity to do for yourself. The success you have in your recovery and continuation is up to you. It is a matter of believing in yourself and your personal resiliencies as you move forward.

As you draw on your own strengths, you may discover that you are able to do a better job of establishing long-term goals. You may also discover the ability to create a more unified philosophy of life, freeing you to make stronger choices in the midst of uncertainty.

Resiliencies are those personal character traits that you employ to help you bounce back after disappointment or tragedy. An exercise that many have found useful is to make a list of personal character traits you have used in the past to successfully face difficulties. Once you have identified those character traits, the next step is to ask how you might be able to access and employ them in your current situation. This process can be very enlightening and empowering as you affirm your ability to deal successfully with difficulties.

Remember, you are the one in charge of your life. You will determine whom and what to add to your suitcase as you travel. You possess what it takes to map out your journey through Good Mourning.

Closing Thoughts

The death of a loved one is life's most crushing blow. You have demonstrated your desire to mourn this loss and move on in healthy ways by reading this book. I believe that you have the resources to successfully work through this painful and difficult time in your life and emerge a stronger person. It will not come easily. You must work at it; however, you are not alone. There are many individuals and resources available to assist you.

I am hopeful that the information presented in this book has been helpful and that you will refer to it over and again as you work through your grief. In summary, I would like to leave you with the following thoughts:

1. **Life Can Be Good!** Your life is and will be different; however, different does not have to mean worse. Different is simply *different*! You can have a meaningful and productive life despite your loss. Begin now to dream about what you desire your good life to be. Make those dreams your life goal.

2. **People Do Create Good Lives!** *You* are responsible for how you respond to what happens in your life. Once you have created goals for your good life, begin formulating plans to make those goals a reality. Form some very specific and measurable steps by which you will accomplish your goals, then work toward your goals and live your dream each day.

3. **You Are the Key!** If you find that things are not working according to your plans or intents, trust yourself and your abilities enough to shift gears and make changes in your approach. Work at eliminating why questions when your plan does not work. Instead, ask, "What can I do differently to accomplish what I want?" As you

keep this attitude, you may find others more willing to assist you as you move forward.

Awaken to Good Mourning!

Finding healthy and useful ways to mourn the death of friends or loved ones is difficult work. Throughout my professional life, I have always found tremendous challenge and reward working with those facing the pain of loss.

Following Christy's death, I was even more aware of how important it is to have tools and resources available to support grieving individuals and families. It was for this reason that *Awaken to Good Mourning* was written.

The information I have shared springs from my own journey through loss and mourning. Because of my experiences, I am more empathetic toward people than I have ever been, and at the same time, I am more hopeful that healthy grief work and grief reconciliation can be realities. There are so many restrictions placed on the bereaved by society, family, friends, and sometimes, self — restrictions that tend to create bad mourning. Too many people become stuck in bad mourning experiences. That is why I want you and others like you to realize that there can be Good Mourning as well.

As I reflect on my life so far, I can truly say that I am thankful I discovered Good Mourning. I now have a new life, a new career, a different kind of family, and new horizons to explore. I have reconciled myself to this loss and integrated it into the fabric of who I am.

Have I forgotten my previous life? Not at all! I have been able to take the lessons from my past, merge them with the experiences of the present, and work toward a future filled with hope and fulfillment. I am learning the power of living in the present tense. I fully know the benefits of Good Mourning and have seen it work for others as well.

Take this challenge life has given you and make it positive. Today, I urge you to raise the blinds of your eyes, open the windows of your soul, and Awaken to Good Mourning!

Take Practical Steps

The work of Good Mourning requires that you take practical steps toward your recovery. At the end of this book, you will find four appendices containing guidelines and resources to help you take those steps.

Appendix A is a checklist of contacts that need to be made in the early part of your mourning experience. These contacts relate to the settlement of estate matters, insurance matters, Social Security, and the like. This section can be used as a guide to help you settle the affairs of your loved one.

Appendix B is a list of books and other written resources available to assist you and your family in dealing with the grief process. Listings are divided according to the specific challenges facing adults, adolescents, and children. As you finish this book, you may want to find other support books as well and develop your own personal library based on your needs and the needs of your family. My hope is that this book will be just the beginning of your written resource collection as you begin a healthy journey to recovery.

Appendix C contains a list of support organizations related to specific types of loss. You may be able to use this list as a beginning point to determine which support groups and organizations exist in your particular area of the country. As you find the groups that have chapters in your area, you may have an easier time becoming involved in appropriate support activities.

Appendix D is designed to help you outline important resources upon which to call as well as assist you in setting goals for expanding these resources in the future. This section consists of personal worksheets to help you organize the necessary contacts to be made and the community support organizations or individuals to be added to your network. A second set of worksheets devoted to the establishment of a dynamic Life Plan is also included. I encourage you to sit down with a trusted friend, advisor, or family member to obtain additional input as you complete these worksheets.

Dealing with First Things — Important Contacts

During the Early Mourning Phase, you will find yourself in a state of flux. This can be a very strange and frightening time in your life. It is important, however, that you make certain initial contacts in the process. If you have already initiated the contacts discussed below, wonderful! If you have yet to make them, then you will want to be sure to do so as soon as possible. If you feel that you are unable to make these contacts alone then you may want to enlist a trusted friend or relative to help. Making these contacts and the necessary decisions that accompany them may open the door for you to begin mourning your loss in healthy ways, and it will help ease you into continuing with your life from this point forward. There are lined worksheets in Appendix D for use in creating a resource list of the people you need to contact. Do not hesitate to make copies of these worksheets if you need to.

Contact an Attorney

Making legal contact will provide a source of advice on such matters as:

- recording property deeds

- taking care of any stocks or bonds your loved one may have owned

- determining the disposition of savings accounts

- organizing the conservation or disbursement of the assets of the estate of your loved one

- managing any business assets

- drawing up a will for the surviving spouse or other family members

If you do not have a family attorney, the local **bar association can assist you with referrals. Friends and** family members can also be an important source of referrals.

If your loved one had a will, obtain a copy as soon as possible. Once the will has been located, take it to your attorney so that he or she can begin filing the necessary legal documents for the probate process. Probate does not have to take a tremendously long time, although each case will vary in complexity. Your attorney will walk you through the process as painlessly as possible. Once the will has been processed, you may distribute the assets of the estate to the beneficiaries as specified by the will.

If your loved one had no will, it is still very important to contact an attorney, because the disposition of the estate can become a more complicated process. From the time the court appoints an administrator of the estate until the estate's final distribution, competent legal counsel is vital. Whether the estate is large or small, covered by a will or not, it is important to contact an attorney so that all legal matters can be handled properly. This course of action may ultimately provide you with some peace of mind, allowing you to focus your full attention on the process of mourning your loss.

If you have lost a child or sibling, it may not be as necessary to contact an attorney. But every situation is different, so simply asking questions regarding whether or not you should obtain legal counsel is a wise choice.

Look for Important Papers

Often, individuals will have left instructions about where to locate important papers. If this was the case with your loved one, you are fortunate in that the search will not be as difficult. If your loved one did not leave instructions, then you must make a thorough search for such documents. Places you might want to look are: safe-deposit boxes, briefcases, home and office desks, strongboxes, safes, lockers, shoe boxes, cedar chests, file cabinets, etc.

Be on the lookout for the following:

- life insurance, disability income, accident and sickness policies

- business agreements

- notes receivable and payable

- securities certificates

- bankbooks

- deeds to real estate

- property lease agreements

- wills or codicils to wills

- copies of recent income tax returns

- W-2 forms and other similar records of earnings

- your loved one's Social Security number

- birth and marriage certificates

- military discharge papers or a Veterans Administration claim number

- automobile registration certificates

- installment payment books

- certificates of membership in professional organizations

- computer program access passwords

The list above is merely representative but should provide you with a great place to begin your search. A word of caution is in order here: Do not discard any official-looking documents! Everything you find could have some potential importance in settling the affairs of your loved one.

Obtain Multiple Copies of the Death Certificate

Making sure that you have an adequate number of copies of the death certificate is important because the death certificate is the basic document with which you will be working as you settle the affairs of your loved one and make any claims to benefits that are rightfully yours. You will need several copies in order to establish claims on life insurance policies, veterans' benefits, and Social Security benefits. You may also be required to present copies to credit card companies to make claims for credit life insurance on accounts or to have your loved one's name removed from accounts.

Often your funeral director can secure certified copies of the certificate for you. If this is not the case, you may obtain copies for a nominal fee from the office of the clerk or registrar in the town, village, or county in which your loved one lived. Remember that a photocopy will not be adequate because it does not bear the raised registrar's or clerk's seal that verifies the document as valid and legal.

Contact Your Life Insurance Agent or Home Office

Generally, life insurance companies only require a statement of claim and a death certificate or statement from the attending physician in order to establish proof of your claim. However, life insurance companies do reserve the right to request additional information or proof if deemed necessary in a given situation.

All life insurance claims should include the following information:

- Policy number(s) and face amount(s)

- Your loved one's full name and address

- The occupation of your loved one and the date he or she last worked (if applicable)

- Your loved one's date and place of birth and the source from which this information was obtained (usually the birth certificate or official hospital record)

- The date, place, and cause of death (taken from the death certificate)

- The claimant's or beneficiary's name, age, address, and Social Security number

The following list details some additional information your insurance company might require for a claim on any insurance policy held in the name of your loved one:

- If the death was associated with an illness, they may ask you to disclose the date when your loved one's health first began to deteriorate.

- If the death occurred strictly from bodily injuries, you might need to indicate whether the injuries and death were the result of an accident, suicide, or homicide.

- They may ask you to provide the name and address of each physician who treated your loved one during the five years prior to his or her death.

- They may ask you to verify who was in possession of the policy at the time of death.

- They may ask you to provide the name of the executor or administrator if one is appointed.

- They may also ask you to provide information — company name, face amount, and date — concerning any other life insurance policies that may have been in force on your loved one at the time of death.

If you or other beneficiaries elect to receive payment of the benefit through one of the optional payment plans, you will need to indicate which payment option you have elected. (The next section, "Options for **Payment of the Benefit,"** offers more information related to payment plans and how they work).

Options for Payment of the Benefit

Life insurance proceeds are generally intended to provide a sense of security and continuity for the beneficiary. After you receive the benefits of the policy, you will have to decide what you want to do with them. Unfortunately, this comes at a time when you are probably the least able or prepared to make such decisions. You may face an additional problem if the amount is a much larger sum of money than you are accustomed to handling. You might feel guilty about receiving the money from an insurance policy and feel an urge to spend the money as quickly as possible. You may also not be aware of how your loved one planned to support you in case something happened to him or her.

The best advice in a situation where life insurance proceeds are involved is that you make no decisions under duress or pressure—either internal or external. Give yourself time to contemplate how your life has changed and what you need to do now in order to move toward securing your future. You will need time to seek counsel from your financial advisors and evaluate your changed financial situation.

All insurance companies have a variety of settlement options available. Although the programs may vary slightly from one company to another, they are essentially the same. The most common settlement options fall into the following categories:

1. Interest Only—In this option, the principal amount of the proceeds remains with the insurance company and the interest is paid periodically to you or another designated party. Usually, provisions can be made to have the right to unlimited withdrawal of funds at any time.

2. Life Income or Annuity—In this option, the company will guarantee to pay you or other beneficiaries a predetermined amount on a set date for the lifetime of the beneficiary/beneficiaries.

3. Fixed Installments—This option provides payment of benefits according to your needs or the needs of other designated beneficiaries in agreed-upon amounts over an agreed-upon term. You or other designated beneficiaries determine the amount of each payment and the duration of payments. This arrangement is similar to a schedule of regular paychecks.

4. Access or Interest-Bearing Checking—In this payment option, the company places the benefits in an account on which checks may be written by you or other designated parties on an as-needed basis. There is generally a minimum balance

that must be maintained and a minimum amount for each check written. In most cases, settlements of $10,000 or more will be placed in an account of this type until a payment option is officially determined. Settlements less than $10,000 are typically distributed in a lump-sum payment. If the amount is less than $10,000 and you desire another type of payment option, you must speak with your agent.

Settlement options can be a valuable tool as you work to create stability for yourself and any other dependents. Consider each option carefully and be sure to ask the advice of your agent or other financial advisor(s). They are capable of assisting you in evaluating your needs and coming up with a plan to best suit your situation.

Contact the Social Security Office

This can be one of the most important contacts of all. There is a lump-sum death benefit of up to $255 for which you may be eligible. In addition, you or other members of your family may be eligible for long-term benefits. Remember, Social Security benefits are not automatic. You must apply for them. You might want to consider making an appointment with the nearest Social Security office so they can begin reviewing your loved one's records before you meet with them. You may save additional time when applying for these benefits by taking the following information to the Social Security office:

- Proof of death (death certificate)

- Your loved one's Social Security number — the actual card, if possible

- The approximate earnings of your loved one in the year in which the death occurred, and the name of his or her employer (a record of these earnings for the year prior to the death is also suggested)

- A copy of the marriage certificate (if the deceased was your spouse)

- The Social Security numbers of the surviving spouse and/or any dependent children

- Proof of age of the surviving spouse and any dependent children under the age of twenty-three

For more information regarding the application for Social Security benefits, please visit their Web site at www.ssa.gov.

Railroad Worker's Benefits

If your loved one worked for the railroads for ten or more years, then Railroad Retirement rather than Social Security will provide the benefits. The Social Security Administration is equipped to provide you with the information necessary to apply for benefits under the Railroad Retirement Act; however, you may also visit their Web site at www.rrb.gov for more information.

Civil Service Benefits

If the deceased was your spouse at the time of death and he or she died in the service after at least eighteen months on the job, then you are entitled to a survivor's annuity, provided you were either married at least two years before the death or are the father or mother of children by the marriage. Additional factors may apply to your individual situation. It is best to make contact with the U.S. Office of Personnel Management for additional details and information.

You may acquire additional information by visiting their Web site at www.opm.gov or calling (202) 606-1800.

Veterans Benefits

If your loved one was a veteran, a range of benefits may be rightfully yours, such as funds that may be applied toward funeral expenses, an American flag for the casket, Dependency and Indemnity Compensation Payments, potential pension payments, and educational financial aid assistance. In order to determine whether you qualify for any of the benefits provided, you must contact the DVA Center. The Web site for the U.S. Department of Veterans Affairs is www.vba.va.gov.

Organizations in Which Your Loved One Held Membership

It is important that you contact any unions, service clubs or organizations, automobile clubs, or professional groups to which your loved one belonged to determine whether you are eligible for any benefits connected with membership. Inquire about the group's life insurance policies that might have been in force at the time of death, any unused portions of annual fees or dues, and special funds or provisions that might be available for the families of deceased members. You never know what additional assistance might be available unless you ask.

Employer and/or Business Associates

Be sure to contact your loved one's place of employment and/or his business associates as soon as possible. Most company employees are covered by group insurance policies of some kind. You must inquire about any benefits due you and the procedure required in filing a claim. You should also ask about retirement and pension fund benefits, any accrued sick pay and vacation time that might carry monetary value, terminal pay allowances, service recognition awards, gratuity payments, unpaid commissions, disability income allowances, credit union balances, and so forth.

You would also be wise to pay particular attention to your loved one's major medical, surgical, disability, and dental coverage to determine whether you and/or your dependents are still eligible for coverage, and if so, for how long and at what cost for continuation.

Mortgage or Credit Life Insurance

Many loans, mortgages, or credit cards are covered by insurance that will pay off the outstanding balance in the event of the death of the borrower. Contact the company or bank in question to inform them of the death of your loved one and ask if such insurance existed. If this coverage was in effect, you need to obtain information about how to proceed with the claim process. These companies will assist you in completing the necessary paperwork and filing the claim.

Wrongful Death Benefits

When there is a possibility that the death was the result of negligent or criminal behavior on the part of another person or company, consult an experienced attorney immediately. It could be less stressful for you to resolve any possibilities of this nature through investigation rather than have unanswered questions cluttering your thinking and feeling processes. An attorney will be able to guide you through the proper procedure for any investigations deemed necessary.

Beware — Some Cautions!

These cautions are especially pertinent for those of you who will be receiving an inheritance or insurance settlement of some kind. The situation in which you find yourself is a very delicate one. Things are not what they used to be. Sometimes there are unscrupulous people who prey upon those who are mourning the death of a loved one. This is unfortunate but true. If you are not careful, you can become the victim of con artists, opportunists, and freeloaders. There are three areas where you can be easily victimized if you are not careful:

Obituary Chasers

If you suddenly find yourself with more money than you have ever had due to an insurance benefit or inheritance, please be aware that there are other people who assume that there will be money available as well. There are companies and individuals who watch the obituaries, take note of the names of survivors, research pertinent contact information, wait a month or so for the disbursement of the benefit to be finalized, and then contact you with the "investment opportunity of a lifetime."

Unless you are aware of this practice, you might think that your funeral director or life insurance agent passed your name on to these vultures. I suggest that you place your trust in financial counselors and advisors you know rather than individuals who offer you "incredible" deals. Again, realize that these folks are out for their own gain and are very resourceful at getting what they want. Be careful!

Hasty Decisions

Sometimes you will be your own worst enemy. There will be times when you feel compelled for various reasons to make a quick decision concerning selling property, moving to a new location, getting rid of assets, making loans to friends or family members, or buying things you really don't need. Instead of acting impulsively on a whim, slow down and take your time. A wise suggestion has been made concerning individuals living in the aftermath of the death of a loved one: If at all possible, make no major decisions for at least six months following the death. This is especially true where financial matters are concerned. Employing the assistance of an advisor or counselor can serve as a buffer from the tyranny of those things that appear urgent in nature. Filtering those situations through another set of eyes, ears, and perceptions may circumvent your making decisions that you might later regret.

Freeloaders

Sometimes after the death of a loved one, survivors discover that many "good friends" and "favorite relatives," whom they have not seen in quite some time, suddenly appear on the scene. The same may be true for you as well. These folks are likely to act in supportive and helpful ways as you make necessary adjustments to life without your loved one; however, that is not always the case.

Please be aware that some of these people might try to convince you to make loans or share your resources for various "necessities" they have. You are particularly vulnerable during this time and may easily find yourself agreeing to give money away or make loans to people when you really need to be focusing on taking care of yourself. Work at making sure you do not allow your financial situation to become public knowledge. Your financial status is a private matter.

This is not to say that you are not free to help family members when they really need the help, provided you are both willing and able to agree to terms and conditions for the help they seek. Just be sure that you do not "help" yourself into more serious problems by falling victim to unnecessary requests for assistance from those closest to you. Remember that any financial assets you have are for you and your immediate dependents, should you have any. You are not a bank. Do not allow people to treat you as if you are one.

Ultimately, the protection of your privacy and personal assets must **take top priority. Your emotional health and well-being is directly tied to this protection.**

Written Resources

The following list of written resources is by no means exhaustive. It merely represents the resources I know of that others have found useful. Reading any of these resources may help you or a family member in your personal journey through Good Mourning.

Books for Adults

A Child's View of Grief: A Guide for Parents, Teachers, and Counselors, *by Alan D. Wolfelt, PhD*

A Grief Observed, *by C. S. Lewis*

Affairs in Order: A Complete Resource Guide to Death and Dying, *by Patricia Anderson*

A Grief Like No Other: Surviving the Violent Death of Someone You Love, *by Kathleen O'Hara*

A Handbook for Widowers, *by Ed Ames*

Beyond Grief: A Guide for Recovering from the Death of a Loved One, *by Carol Staudacher*

Beyond Widowhood: From Bereavement to Emergence and Hope, *by Robert C. Digiulio*

Death and the Family: The Importance of Mourning, *by Lily Pincus*

Don't Take My Grief Away: What to Do When You Lose a Loved One, *by Doug Manning*

Explaining Death to Children, *by Earl A. Grollman*

Finding Your Way When Your Spouse Dies, *by Linus Mundy*

Five Cries of Grief, *by Merton P. Strommen and A. Irene Strommen*

Going On . . . A Pathway Through Sorrow, *by Jane Woods Shoemaker*

Good Grief, *by Granger E. Westberg*

Help Your Marriage Survive the Death of a Child, *by Paul Rosenblatt*

How to Go On Living When Someone You Love Dies, *by Therese A. Rando*

I'm Grieving as Fast as I Can: How Young Widows and Widowers Cope and Heal, *by Linda Feinberg*

Men and Grief: A Guide for Men Surviving the Death of a Loved One, *by Carol Staudacher*

No Time for Goodbyes: Coping with Sorrow, Anger, and Injustice After a Tragic Death, *by Janice Harris Lord*

Seven Choices: Taking the Steps to New Life After Losing Someone You Love, *by Elizabeth Harper Neeld*

Starting Over: Help for Young Widows and Widowers, *by Adele Rice Nudel*

Talking About Death: A dialogue Between Parent and Child, *by Earl A. Grollman*

The Grief Recovery Handbook: A Step-by-Step Program for Moving Beyond Loss, *by John W. James & Frank Cherry*

The Heart of Grief: Death and the Search for Lasting Love, *by Thomas Attig*

The Loss That Is Forever: The Lifelong Impact of the Early Death of a Mother or Father, *by Maxine Harris*

Tough Transitions: Navigating Your Way Through Difficult Times, *by Elizabeth Harper Neeld*

When Bad Things Happen to Good People, *by Harold S. Kushner*

When Someone You Love Completes Suicide, by Sondra Sexton-Jones

When Winter Follows Spring: Surviving the Death of an Adult Child, *by Dorothy Ferguson*

Books for Teens

A Taste of Blackberries, *by Doris Buchanan Smith and Michael Wimmer*

After Suicide: Living with the Questions, *by Eileen Kuehn*

Circle of Gold, *by Candy Dawson Boyd*

Coping With the Death of a Brother or Sister, *by Ruth Ann Ruiz*

Facing Change: Falling Apart and Coming Together Again in the Teen Years, *by Donna B. O'Toole*

Fire in My Heart, Ice in My Veins: A Journal for Teenagers Experiencing Loss, *by Enid Samuel Traisman*

Healing Your Grieving Heart for Teens: 100 Practical Ideas, *by Alan D. Wolfelt, PhD*

Help for the Hard Times, *by Earl Hipp*

Helping Teens Work Through Grief, *by Mary Kelly Perschy*

How It Feels When a Parent Dies, *by Jill Krementz*

Mick Harte Was Here, *by Barbara Park*

Reactions: A Workbook to Help Young People Who Are Experiencing Trauma and Grief, *by Alison Salloum*

Straight Talk about Death for Teenagers: How to Cope with Losing Someone You Love, *by Earl A. Grollman*

Common Threads of Teenage Grief, *by Janet Tyson*

The Day I Saw My Father Cry, *by Bill Cosby*

The Grieving Teen: A Guide for Teenagers and Their Friends, *by Helen Fitzgerald*

You Are Not Alone: Teens Talk About Life After the Loss of a Parent, *by Lynne B. Hughes*

Books for Children

Helping Children Heal from Loss: A Keepsake Book of Special Memories, *by Laurie Van-Si & Lynn Powers*

A Terrible Thing Happened, *by Margaret M. Holmes and Sasha J. Mudlaff*

A Volcano in My Tummy: Helping Children to Handle Anger, *by Eliane Whitehouse and Warwick Pudney*

Aarvy Aardvark Finds Hope, *by Donna R. O'Toole*

After a Murder: A Workbook for Grieving Kids, *by the Dougy Center*

Am I Still a Sister? *by Alicia M. Sims*

What Is Cancer Anyway: Explaining Cancer to Children of All Ages, *by Karen L. Carney*

Children Also Grieve: Talking about Death and Healing, *by Linda Goldman*

Coping With the Death of a Brother or Sister, *by Ruth Ann Ruiz*

Life and Death in the Third Grade, *by Maureen A. Burns and Cara Burns*

Lifetimes: A Beautiful Way to Explain Death to Children, *by Bryan Mellonie and Robert R. Ingpen*

Nana Upstairs & Nana Downstairs, *by Tomie dePaola*

One More Wednesday, *by Malika Doray*

Something from Nothing, *by Phoebe Gilman*

Sunflowers and Rainbows for Tia: Saying Goodbye to Daddy, *by Alesia K. Alexander*

The Butterfly Field, *by Alquin Glaini*

The Fall of Freddie the Leaf, *by Leo Buscaglia, PhD*

The Memory Box, *by Kirsten McLaughlin*

The Sun and Spoon, *by Kevin Henkes*

When Dinosaurs Die: A Guide to Understanding Death, *by Laurie Kransy Brown and Marc Brown*

APPENDIX: C

Support Organizations

Below is a representative list of support organizations with information and resources which might be useful to you or your family. Many organizations have local chapters, and you can locate them on the Web sites listed. Most of these organizations also provide printed materials; many are free of charge. Check out the Web sites to determine which groups may best satisfy your information needs.

AARP — www.aarp.org/family/lifeafterloss

AIDS Project Los Angeles — www.apla.org

American Association of Suicidology — www.suicidology.org

American SIDS Institute — www.sids.org

Association for Death Education and Counseling — www.adec.org

Bereaved Families of Ontario — www.bereavedfamilies.net

Center for Loss and Life Transition — www.centerforloss.com

Centering Corporation — www.centering.org

Comfort Zone Camp — www.comfortzonecamp.org

Compassionate Friends — www.compassionatefriends.org

Grief Net — www.griefnet.org

Kids Cope with Grief — www.kidscopewithgrief.com

Kid Said — www.kidsaid.com

Loved Ones Victims Services — www.lovs.org

National Center for Victims of Crime — www.ncvc.org

National Organization of Parents of Murdered Children — www.pomc.com

Parents Without Partners — www.parentswithoutpartners.org

Society of Military Widows — www.militarywidows.org

The Children's Room — www.childrensroom.org

The Dougy Center – www.grievingchild.org

The Journey of Hope Grief Support Center — www.johgriefsupport.org

The W.A.R.M. (What About Remembering Me) Place — www.thewarmplace.org

Widow Net — www.widownet.org

Personal Worksheets — Expanding Community Support

The following set of worksheets can help you organize and categorize potential community support resources as they exist in your specific area. Space is provided for you to list names, phone numbers, and addresses as you work through each category. You will also find space for listing resource needs unique to you and your situation. I encourage you to sit down with a friend as you evaluate these community support resources. This collaboration can ensure a more complete listing for your continued reference.

Step One: Potential Community Support Resources

In this step, you will begin listing all the possible sources of support that exist in your community. For some of the categories listed, you may already have relationships established. Go ahead and list those established contacts as you work through this section. You may find that listing already established contacts can serve as a catalyst to bring to mind other resources as well.

Your Life Insurance Agent and/or Company

Name_____ Phone_____

Address_____

Name_____ Phone_____

Address_____

Name_____ Phone_____

Address_____

Financial Advisors and Investment Counselors

Name_____ Phone_____

Address_____

Name_____ Phone_____

Address_____

Name_____ Phone_____

Address_____

Church/Temple/Synagogue Contacts

Name_____ Phone_____

Address_____

Name_____ Phone_____

Address_____

Name_____ Phone_____

Address_____

Physicians

Name_____ Phone_____

Address_____

Name_____ Phone_____

Address_____

Name_____ Phone_____

Address_____

Hospital Contacts

Name_____ Phone_____

Address_____

Name_____ Phone_____

Address_____

Name_____ Phone_____

Address_____

Professional Therapists and Counselors

Name_____ Phone_____

Address_____

Name_____ Phone_____

Address_____

Name_____ Phone_____

Address_____

Attorney or Legal Counsel Resources

Name_____ Phone_____

Address_____

Name_____ Phone_____

Address_____

Name_____ Phone_____

Address_____

Support Group Contacts

Name_____ Phone_____

Address_____

Name_____ Phone_____

Address_____

Name_____ Phone_____

Address_____

Health Clubs and Spas

Name_____ Phone_____

Address_____

Name_____ Phone_____

Address_____

Name_____ Phone_____

Address_____

Home and/or Yard Maintenance

Name_____ Phone_____

Address_____

Name_____ Phone_____

Address_____

Name_____ Phone_____

Address_____

Books/Music/CDs

Title_____

Title_____

Title_____

Title_____

Title_____

Title_____

Volunteer Organizations

Name_____ Phone_____

Address_____

Name_____ Phone_____

Address_____

Name_____ Phone_____

Address_____

Additional Resources

Name_____ Phone_____

Address_____

Name_____ Phone_____

Address_____

Name_____ Phone_____

Address_____

Step Two: Possible Additions to Your Personal Support System

After studying the compiled list, analyze your personal needs and select five resources not currently a part of your personal support system and write them in the space provided. This step helps narrow your focus to those resources you most likely need to add to your list of easily accessible support, information, or guidance.

1. _____

2. _____

3. _____

4. _____

5. _____

Step Three: Building an Action Plan

Finally, from the list of five possible additions, develop a basic, three-step action plan to determine exactly how these people or resources will be added to your community support system. Be sure to include specific timeframes for completing each addition. Specific timeframes can help keep you focused on the tasks at hand. For example, you might write something like: "I will add a grief support group to my community support system by referring to Appendix C in this book to find a chapter in my area, and I will do so within the next two weeks."

A.   I will add _____ **to my community support** system by_____ within the next

_____.

B.   I will add _____ **to my community support**

system by_____ within the next

_____.

C.   I will add _____ **to my community support**

system by_____ within the next

_____.

D.   I will add _____ **to my community support**

system by_____ within the next

_____.

E.   I will add _____ **to my community support**

system by_____ within the next

_____.

This progression of activities can now become a framework for creating a plan to access community support for your continued growth through this process. I encourage you to periodically refer to your lists and update them as necessary.

Personal Worksheets — Creation of a Life Plan

The development of a Life Plan involves the following distinct aspects: your overall dream or goal, your statement of purpose or intent, your strategy or action steps, and your measure of progress. I suggest that you copy these pages and use one set per individual goal, dream, or project. This will help you keep track of your progress toward each part of your Life Plan.

Step One Asks: *What Do You Want to Do?*

In this step, state what you want to do, become, have, accomplish, or establish — the goal or dream toward which you want to work. In essence, you are completing the statement, *I want to:*

_____

_____

_____

_____

_____

_____

_____

_____

_____

_____

_____

Step Two Asks: *What Are the Parts of Your Dream or Goal?*

The second step involves breaking down your dream into its various parts. This step becomes the establishment of your statements of purpose or intent. You become more specific as you clarify each part of your goal. You will take each part of your overall goal and begin breaking it down to its necessary components. You essentially complete the statement, *In order to* _____, *I must:*

_____

_____

_____

_____

_____

_____

_____

_____

_____

_____

_____

Step Three Asks: *What Strategies Will You Employ, or What Action Steps Will You Take?*

As you work this part of the process, consider the steps you will need to take to make your statement(s) of purpose a reality. *How much time or money will it require? What other resources or support do I need in order to accomplish my purpose? What known obstacles exist that I can address at the beginning of my project?* Essentially, you complete the statement, ***As I pursue*** _____, ***I will need to:***

_____

_____

_____

_____

_____

_____

_____

_____

_____

_____

Step Four Asks: *How Will You Measure Your Progress?*

The fourth and final step in the development of your Life Plan focuses on measuring your progress. This step involves keeping track of your progress as you work your Life Plan. It causes you to ask such questions as: *How will I know whether I have attained this particular part of my plan? What do I need to do differently to reach my goal if one strategy should fail? How does my strategy need to be altered?* This step will help you to check your progress, reminding you that you are in control of your responses and choices as you move forward. Essentially, you are completing the following statement: ***I will monitor my progress toward this goal by setting the following parameters and measures:***

_____

_____

_____

_____

_____

_____

_____

_____

_____

Made in the USA
Coppell, TX
19 December 2021